The Testament of Amram

(The Father of Moses)

"I saw Watchers in my dream vision...
Two were fighting over me. I asked [one], 'Who are you?'...

He answered me, 'We have been empowered and rule over all mankind. Which of us do you choose to rule you?'"...

One of them was terrifying in his appearance...
his visage like a viper. I asked, 'Who is he?'

He answered me, 'This Watcher has three names — Belial, Prince of Darkness and King of Evil. He is empowered over all darkness, while I am empowered over all light...
and over all that is of God.'

I asked him, 'What are your names?'

He said, 'My three names are Michael, and Prince of Light and King of Righteousness.'"

From *The Dead Sea Scrolls*

"In a very interesting and entertaining way Joe Lewels has woven together hypnotic regression work regarding past lives and current life extraterrestrial encounters with scholarly research into the origin of Christianity. This is a truly fascinating read about who we really are and what it means to be here in Earth life."

— Barbara Lamb, psychotherapist (retired)
and CHT Regression Therapist, author and speaker
barbaralambregression.com

"...there is much truth in Lewels's historical and biblical analysis. I believe the issues in this book will eventually come to dominate religious discussion for decades to come."

—Barry H. Downing is Pastor Emeritus of Northminster Presbyterian Church, Endwell, NY. Author of *The Bible and Flying Saucers* in 1968 and *Biblical UFO Revelations*.
https://thebibleandflyingsaucers.com/about/

See more comments by Rev. Downing
in the Preface

"This is a 'must-read' book, as the possibility of the ETs making more open contact on Earth looms larger on the horizon, with tentative expectations for within the next five years. Joe Lewels, Ph.D., has been investigating ET-contact experiences since 1993, working with a team of psychiatrists and hypnotherapists. He is a certified hypnotherapist with the American Institute of Hypnotherapy, and he has interviewed hundreds of experiencers of ET contact in the U.S., Australia and Mexico. He prefers to use the term "experiencers" rather than "abductees", as he has found that most do not feel that they are victims, but rather participants, who have made a pre-birth choice to be part of the awakening and evolutionary process being carried out by higher-dimensionals such as the so-called Greys. I find very many parallels between his findings and my own lifelong contact experiences with these Beings."

— Judy Carroll, author of *The Zeta Message,*
Human by Day, Zeta by Night:
Extraterrestrial Presence on Earth,
Cosmic Spirituality, and
An Interview with an Alien.
ufogreyinfo.com

©2025 by Joe Lewels
All rights reserved. No part of this book may be reproduced in any form or by any electronic or mechanical means including information and retrieval systems without prior permission from the publisher in writing.

print ISBN: 978-0-926524-04-0
E-book ISBN: 978-0-926524-05-7

Library of Congress Control Number
2025913093

Subject Classifications: Extraterrestrials, Ancient Religions, Dead Sea Scrolls, Hypnotherapy, Past Life Regression

Manuscript Editors:
Brian L. Crissey, Pamela Meyer
Manuscript & Cover Design:
Pamela Meyer and Brian L. Crissey

The ET on the front cover
created by ChatGPT

The Soul Trap

Aliens, Ancient Scrolls and Reincarnation

Joe Lewels, Ph.D.

Wild Flower Press
an imprint of Granite Publishing, L.L.C.
P.O. Box 338
Mt. Pleasant, SC 29464

Dedicated to Hilda,
the love of my life.

Contents

Preface by Rev. Barry Downing ix

Introduction xi

Editor's Note xv

Section I	**The Journey Begins**	**xvii**
Chapter 1	"We Recycle Souls"	1
Chapter 2	"I Ran Back to the Church"	7
Chapter 3	Mack Attack	15
Chapter 4	Healing Wounds, Finding Purpose	26
Chapter 5	The Cosmic Coffee Table	35
Section II	**Ancient Connections**	**41**
Chapter 6	The River Lethe	42
Chapter 7	The Essenes	47
Chapter 8	The Watchers	62
Chapter 9	Jesus: Man or God?	66
Chapter 10	The Gnostics	76
Chapter 11	The War on Reincarnation	86
Chapter 12	The Inquisition	96
Chapter 13	Regulating Karma	101
Chapter 14	The Masters	105
Chapter 15	The Andreasson Affair	110

Section III	Confirmation	**115**
Chapter 16	The Tall Blondes	116
Chapter 17	Confirmation	129
Chapter 18	The Cosmic Game Wardens	133
Chapter 19	The Custodians	138
Chapter 20	Jesus and the Essenes	142
Chapter 21	A Purposeful Universe	152
Chapter 22	Miracle in Mexico	157
Chapter 23	The Reptilians	166

Section IV	Hidden Truths	**173**
Chapter 24	The Reptilian Project	174
Chapter 25	The Hunchbacked Woman	182
Chapter 26	Soul Transfers	190
Chapter 27	Scientific and Religious Beliefs	198
Chapter 28	La Vida Es Para Sufrir	205

About the Author
    Dr. Joe Lewels   213

Acknowledgments   215

Index   216

References   221

Preface
Rev. Barry Downing

Joe Lewels and I agree that UFOs are of great scientific and religious significance, and that there has been ET contact for centuries, including during the time of the Bible. We also agree that ETs seem to be interdimensional, not from another planet, and we also agree that we can learn more about ET purpose from human abductions and close encounters than we can from a hundred crashed UFOs. This book is an excellent combination of what we have learned from ET contact, and the history of religion in the West especially, that which has been dominated by Christianity. *I believe the issues in this book will eventually come to dominate religious discussion for decades to come.*

As a trained hypnotherapist who has heard the stories of hundreds of experiencers, Dr. Lewels has formed an opinion about the purpose of human life from the testimony of the experiencers. In a nut shell this is it: Earth is a kind of "Soul Trap," or prison, the purpose of human life is to go through a series of tests, and we have to keep being reincarnated until we "get it right," and move on to heavenly joy and freedom. The ETs manage us as we work our way through our various incarnations.

Lewels makes his main argument in favor of reincarnation and against resurrection in Chapter 9, "Jesus: Man or God?" and Chapter 11, "The War On Reincarnation." His view is that the Church chose resurrection over reincarnation due to a political struggle, during the time of Constantine. I believe there is much truth in Lewels's historical and biblical analysis.

I differ with Lewels theologically, not historically. Jesus preached of a God who loves us, even when we mess up, and we do not earn that love—it is a free gift. The Parable of the Prodigal Son in Luke 15 explains the difference. The Prodigal Son has wasted his father's money, returns home totally broken, and is greeted with a new robe, cleaned up, and the father kills the fatted calf to celebrate the return of his lost son. This is salvation by grace, not by good works. The elder brother complains that "it's not fair," your worthless son comes home to celebration, I have worked hard on your farm all my life, but you have not even given me a goat to celebrate with my friends.

I am willing to suggest that the two brothers represent two paths to salvation from this "Soul Trap," for those who want to work their way up the reincarnation ladder, life after life, go ahead. But if you would rather, when you die, be welcomed with joy into God's house, where all is forgiven, then believe in the God of Jesus.

Jesus is my preferred path, My God.

Introduction

What do you believe happens when you die? I have asked this question to many people—friends, associates, attendees at conferences where I have been a speaker—and I am always surprised that so many people say that nothing happens. "Everything goes black. That's all there is," they say. Such people don't even believe that they have a soul, or that there is anything beyond the physical, material world that they can see and touch. That common reply, I believe, is the result of the failure, not only of our religions, but also of our scientific institutions. The result is that people have no incentive to be good since there is nothing waiting for them in the afterlife.

This dangerous misconception about the true nature of reality is based on the standard used to define the universe we live in—the scientific method. In this book the reader will learn that there is a better way to understand the true nature of reality, and it has nothing to do with the scientific method. If given a chance, this book can help even the most die-hard atheist discover that he does have a soul and there is still time to act to avoid the terrible consequence of remaining trapped in the material world time and time again.

Another common reply, from people who are deeply religious, is that souls go to Heaven or to Hell and remain there for eternity—a horrible notion indeed. This belief is equally dangerous because it only allows humans one chance to make it to Heaven. There are no do-overs. This notion causes many to just give up trying to live the perfect life—a system they see as unfair—and lose their faith in God. But an understanding of the laws of karma and reincarnation teaches us that life is fair and that we have many chances to get to Heaven and avoid the soul trap we know as Planet Earth—the true Hell.

Amazingly there are a growing number of Americans who already understand that reincarnation is real. According to a Pew Research Center study in 2021, 38% of U.S. adults under the age of 50 believe in reincarnation, compared to 27% of adults 50 and older. Young Americans, it seems, are somehow more open to the idea than are older ones, but do they change their opinions once they age? We don't know, but we do know that approximately 60% of Americans identify themselves as Christian, so some of these have strayed from the Church's teachings about the afterlife. What is even more amazing is that the study found Catholics are more likely to believe in reincarnation than are Protestants, with 38% of Catholics saying they believe in it, while only 26% of Protestants do. The findings show that the Church is losing influence among Americans who seem to be finding spiritual teachings from other sources. A few hundred years ago, these people would have been declared to be heretics and would have been arrested, tortured and burned at the stake by "well-meaning" Christians.

I admit that I too am a heretic, and that my book is heretical. It's amazing I found a publisher for my manuscript, for they too would be called heretics. According to Catholic doctrine, a heretic is anyone who believes, teaches, or feels he could have or has had a direct relationship with God, without the authority of the Church, or anyone who is opposed to Catholic doctrine. As the reader will see, many tens of thousands were put to death in the past for teaching or believing in reincarnation. Today, such people don't have to worry about being murdered for their beliefs, but Catholics can be excommunicated and Protestants can be shunned and asked to leave the congregation. I'm not worried about either punishment, as I long ago broke ties with religious teachings and decided to search for spirituality independently. What I discovered was astounding.

This book shares with the reader how to escape the seemingly endless cycle of reincarnation. It is also about the powerful god-like beings who are there in the afterlife to judge us when we die, and who decide what is to be done with us. Because they have monitored our progress, or lack of it, they know every thought we have had and every action we have taken. They are there to decide if we have led righteous lives, and are therefore ready to move on to a higher plane of existence, or if we have more to learn and must go back to planet Earth to be born again as a human—our past-life memories erased. These enormously powerful beings have been called by many names. In the ancient texts, such as the Bible, The Dead Sea Scrolls, the Books of Enoch and the Lost Gospels, they are called the Watchers—beings who rule over life on Earth. Today, many believe they are aliens from outer space.

Whatever we call them, they are real—very real. So real that it is a great mistake to not believe in them. Your soul is at stake. This book is meant to help the reader by exposing him/her to the bountiful evidence that exists, not only in the ancient texts, but in the present world, of their existence. It is the story of my personal journey of self-discovery, having been raised in a Catholic family early in life and then as a Bible-quoting Protestant in my later life. I know both religions well, and I know the Bible. As a member of a Presbyterian congregation that emphasized Bible study from the age of 8 through my college years, I was immersed in Bible study. There was Sunday school just before the service, which included a lengthy sermon delivered mightily by our pastor, Dr. Bennet, who was a Doctor of Theology. He was held in great respect by the congregation as an expert on the Bible.

In the summer there was vacation Bible school, a week-long course for the youth of the church in which our teacher tried to explain the Bible to a bunch of disinterested teenagers. But for some reason, I was not disinterested. I found the Bible fascinating. I listened to the teachers carefully and I asked questions they couldn't answer, such as "Why is God so wrathful in the Old Testament and so kind in the New Testament? Jehovah told the Israelites to massacre the Canaanites, the Jebusites, and all the other "ites" and to even kill the women, children and their animals so they could take over their land. But Jesus taught people to be non-violent and to turn the other cheek. That doesn't make sense."

The teachers had no answer for questions like that, so I quickly concluded that the teachers didn't know what they were talking about. Later in life, through vigorous study of the ancient texts, by organizing a team of experts to conduct an investigation into alien abductions, and by experiencing a past-life hypnotic regression, I was able to understand the truth about the Bible and the religious institutions that use it, perhaps inadvertently, to keep us trapped in the material world. My greatest hope is that you will, at the very least, consider the possibility that you have lived before and will live again. Better yet, I hope my book motivates you to discover your own past lives by finding a qualified hypnotherapist and scheduling a session of past-life regression. What do you have to lose, compared to what you have to gain?

Or perhaps you like the chaos that reigns on planet Earth, and the inevitable pain and suffering that goes along with the experience. It's like my Mexican grandmother used to tell me, "La vida es para sufrír." (Life is for suffering.) I didn't believe her back then when I was a child, but now, in my old age, I realize how wise she was. Life on planet Earth *is* for suffering—that's the whole point.

Editor's Note

Consistency between differing bodies of thought suggests that there must be a common ground supporting both traditions.

But what could that be?

Dr. Lewels finds that the Cathars, the Essenes, the Buddhists, and the Gnostics held similar beliefs. What could these traditions have experienced in their distant past? Could Jesus have been of multidimensional origin, with many traditions having their own memories of His time here?

It is likely that extraterrestrial visitation is a very old process, one dating back to human origins, one that modern Western researchers are just beginning to understand. Far from being the cutting-edge fully knowledgable researchers they profess to be, modern scientists are increasingly seen as needing to catch up with the deeper understanding of human-multidimensional interface that native peoples have quietly demonstrated for centuries.

Almost all indigenous peoples claim to have originated in the stars. Native Americans often hold their off-planet experiences close to the vest, but when they sometimes share them, as they did at the Star Knowledge gathering in South Dakota in 1990, it becomes clear that Jesus may have been right when he said, "So the last will be first, and the first will be last."

Section I

The Journey Begins

1

"We Recycle Souls"

In the summer of 1987 my life took a strange turn. My wife and I were at the Cielo Vista Mall in east El Paso, Texas, about to enter a movie theater for a 7 p.m. show. We always made time to make a brief stop to browse at the Waldenbooks bookstore, which faced the theater. But this time, as we approached, something striking caught my eye and my immediate attention. It was the dust cover of a book depicting the face of a strange, hairless creature with huge, black, almond-shaped, eyes, a tiny nose and a small slit for a mouth. I recognized it at once as the face of an alien, not because I had ever seen one, but because by then most of the world had been exposed to the story of Betty and Barney Hill, a mixed-race couple who claimed to have been abducted by aliens. Their story had been published as a book and made into a television movie called "The Interrupted Journey." By 1987 the world had become familiar with the little Gray aliens with the big black eyes.

Additionally, the 1981 publishing of the book, *Missing Time,* by New York artist Budd Hopkins, revealed an enigma that captured the world of popular culture by introducing the concept of "missing time"—a term now synonymous with alien abductions.

Hopkins followed this book up in 1987 with his book, *Intruders*, which spent four weeks on the New York Times best-sellers list, and was made into a CBS miniseries in 1992.

Waldenbooks had set up a display of the alien-face books at the front of the store where it couldn't be missed by passersby. I took my wife by the arm and guided her into the store. "What's going on?" she asked. "I have to take a look at that book," I replied, pointing at the strange face of an alien. There was just something alluring about that face; I was pulled toward it as if by a magnet. I quickly plucked a copy from the rack and read the words on the cover: "*Communion*, A true story by Whitley Strieber, co-author of *Warday*." The book was autobiographical, a recounting of the author's experiences as someone who had been abducted by aliens.

I was taken aback because I knew this author's work. I had read several of his books including *Warday, Nature's End, The Wolfen* and *The Hunger*. Strieber was a well-es-

tablished author of best-selling novels, as well as books based on solid research about the dangers posed to life on earth by climate change and nuclear proliferation. Two of his books, *The Hunger* and *The Wolfen*, had been made into movies. He was a brilliant, highly- intelligent writer—someone I admired and someone I would get to know well many years later, when I began my own research into the abduction mystery. But at that moment I realized he was taking a huge risk by going public about his experiences. He was most certainly going to be attacked and discredited in the media. He had ventured into dangerous territory.

    I understood his plight well, for I had seen a UFO years earlier when I was a U.S. Army aviator just back from a tour in Vietnam. On a clear night in south Alabama in January 1969, I was on a flight in a single-engine Cessna near the Gulf of Mexico with my boss, a colonel who had also returned recently from the war. It was not a close encounter. A strange, large, orange orb followed us around for more than an hour at a distance, giving us both the chills. When we returned to the base at Fort Rucker, AL, we decided not to report the incident and not to mention it to anyone. We both knew we would face ridicule and our flight status could be in jeopardy if we disclosed what we had experienced. Pilots just knew not to report UFOs back then.

    There was another event in my life that drew me closer to the UFO mystery. In the early 1970s, I had the opportunity to meet and interview Dr. J. Allen Hynek, a highly regarded professor of astronomy, who for many years served as a consultant to the U.S. Air Force's Project Blue Book's investigation into UFOs. He left the project and recanted his bogus explanation of "swamp gas" as it related to multiple UFO sightings by many witnesses in a Michigan case. He admitted publicly that the purpose of the Air Force project was to discredit witnesses and deny the existence of UFOs. In 1975, his book, *The UFO Experience*, was published and the movie rights were quickly purchased by movie producer/

director Stephen Spielberg. This resulted in his 1977 blockbuster movie, "Close Encounters of the Third Kind", in which Hynek served as a consultant, and also made a cameo appearance.

After I told him about my UFO experience, Hynek confided in me something that was not in his book: that one of his confidential sources, an Army colonel, swore to him that a flying disk had crashed near Roswell, NM in 1947, and alien bodies were recovered along with the wreckage. What ensued, Hynek said, was an elaborate government cover up, one that continues to the present day. Hynek then asked me to work as a volunteer investigator for his civilian organization, The Center for UFO Studies (CUFOS), but I declined the invitation because at the time I was a professor of journalism at the University of Texas at El Paso; I was afraid it would damage my reputation. This is why I understood well the trepidation Strieber must have felt when he decided to go public about his contact with aliens.

Even though Strieber's book remained number one on the New York Times non-fiction best-seller list for ten months, and he received thousands of letters from people all over the world saying they too had similar experiences, (see his 2023 book, *Them*, to read some of the correspondence) his open admission to having had contact with aliens would undoubtedly cause a severe backlash. No other famous or high profile celebrity had ever publicly admitted to such a thing. (The exception being actress Shirley McLain, who was ridiculed in the press but somehow managed to continue making great movies.) But the movie business is one thing and the publishing business is quite another. Strieber had risked his entire credibility and career by challenging the scientific paradigm, and that makes publishers nervous. I knew at once that this was an important book; I immediately bought it and took it with me into the theater.

I was terribly excited about getting home and reading Strieber's amazing book, *Communion*, which I devoured in two days; I was flabbergasted. His story about being taken by aliens and having intrusive medical procedures performed on him was more terrifying than the fictional tales he was known for, such as those involving vampires and supernatural wolves. It was frightening to read about how he was mysteriously immobilized, but conscious, and taken from his bed by a cadre of small alien beings, only to wake up the next morning with only fleeting memories of the event. He had known nothing of UFOs and aliens and didn't take much notice of such stories in the news. Despite his talent for writing scary novels about supernatural creatures, in real life he was a spiritual searcher who studied the teachings of George Gurdjieff (1866-1949), a Greek-Armenian spiritual teacher influenced by Sufi, Zen and Yogi Mystics. Gurdjieff taught that humans live in a hypnotic state similar to sleep. To transcend this state and awaken to a state of enlightenment, one had to use a process he taught called "mindfulness," similar to meditation. This allows the person to understand that the soul survives the body after death and reincarnates—something he called "recurrence."

By his early 40s, Strieber, a 1967 graduate of the University of Texas, had taken up meditation and felt he had a good grasp of reality. But even the Gurdjieff system could not have prepared him for what happened in his cabin in the woods on that fateful night when aliens took him away. Despite all his mindfulness training and self-realization, Strieber panicked. He believed he was going crazy (a common reaction among those who experience this phenomenon.) He wanted his experience to be anything but real. Gurdjieff hadn't taught him anything about aliens! Perhaps he had a brain tumor or a psychotic episode, he rationalized. But after enduring psychiatric testing and brain scans, which all confirmed he was healthy and totally sane, he ultimately turned to hypnosis for answers.

With the help of a psychiatrist of high repute, who was known to be well-versed in the use of hypnosis, Strieber was able to recover memories of terrifyingly real events during which he endured painful medical procedures at the hands of very strange-looking, sentient creatures. It was alarming for him to realize he was not crazy, nor was he suffering from some unknown brain disorder. He was forced to reevaluate everything he ever believed to be true about the nature of the universe and of reality itself. Eventually he concluded the strange beings were real, but what were they? And where did they come from? Why did they pick him to torment? He began to refer to them as "Visitors," but soon began to surmise that they may not be just visiting, but rather they had always been part of human existence. "Even if the visitors were real," he wrote, "there was no reason to believe that they were simply creatures from another planet. It could be that the Visitors were really from here. Certainly, the long tradition of fairy lore suggested that something had been with us for far more than 40 or 50 years since the phenomenon took on its present appearance."

He even considered the possibility that they were the gods of ancient mythology or even that they were from a different dimension. One of the notions he considered was that "we are prisoners on our planet." This revelation, perhaps the most disturbing of all, was reinforced by a vivid memory he had of one particular experience with the "visitors" in which they actually answered one of his questions. He remembered blurting out: "Who are you?"

Their cryptic response made his blood run cold:

"We recycle souls." they said.

Chapter 2

"I Ran Back to the Church"

One can hardly blame Strieber for considering that his tormentors might be demons. That is a common conclusion made by people all over the world who experience what is commonly known as the "alien-abduction experience." I should know. I organized a team of psychiatrists and hypnotherapists and began investigating such cases in 1993; I have interviewed hundreds of "abductees" all over the U.S. and even in Mexico and Australia. In 1995 I became certified by the American Institute of Hypnotherapy and have used hypnosis hundreds of times to help people recover missing memories of their alien experiences.

One of the most interesting findings we made was that many "experiencers," as I prefer to call them, do not feel that they are victims, but rather that they actually agreed to being a participant in this strange phenomenon before they incarnated into their present lives. These revelations of having made a contract, or agreement are often accompanied by vivid, past-life and in-between life memories. The agreements occur as they are planning their next life, with the help of higher discarnate alien beings. As bizarre as this sounds, the recovery of such memories helped them to minimize their fears, allowing them to understand they are not victims, but rather participants who actually volunteered to play out this role as "abductee" in their present lives.

Doctors, psychiatrists, professors, corporate executives, nurses, truck drivers, housewives and even a Native American shaman have been among my many cases. The strange phenomenon does not discriminate. Men, women, children, blacks, whites, Mexicans, upper class, lower class, middle class—all are taken. The story of my research project is documented in my two books: *The God Hypothesis: Extraterrestrial Life and its Implications for Science and Religion* (Wildflower Press, 1997, second edition 2005) and *Rulers of the Earth: Secrets of the Sons of God* (Galde Press, 2007.)

The success of my books is due in part to Strieber's generous endorsement, which appeared on the back cover of *The God Hypothesis*. I first met Whitley Strieber at a large UFO conference in Brisbane, Queensland Australia in 1996, just as my first book was about to be published. He and I were among the 20 or so speakers asked to make presentations before an audience of about 500 people from all over Australia and New Zealand. I found myself seated between

JOE LEWELS AND WHITLEY STRIEBER AT BOOK SIGNING IN EL PASO, TX.
(Photo by author)

Strieber and Dr. John Mack, a Harvard professor of psychiatry whose 1994 book, A*bduction: Human Encounters with Aliens*, caused a worldwide sensation. I took the opportunity to ask them to read my manuscript and, if they felt so inclined, to write a blurb for the back cover of the book. It was my good fortune that they both agreed to do so. Strieber sent me the following blurb:

"Finally a book seriously addresses the question of what the possibility of an alien presence does to religion. It's an exciting, pioneering look at what is almost certainly about to become the burning question of the age, indeed all ages."

Obviously, the impact of alien visitations on the religions of the world and on his own religion of Catholicism, weighed heavily on his mind, as it did mine. Early on in my research I began to question the "Extraterrestrial Hypothesis" proposed by other researchers. What I discovered in my research seemed to me to be something other than an alien or ET invasion of Planet Earth. What kind of extraterrestrial visitors might possess such astounding abilities as those described by individuals who have encountered them directly?

In the many cases I have studied, the beings are reported to communicate primarily telepathically, rather than by the spoken word. They disguise their presence by planting "screen" memories in the sub-conscious minds of the "participants," thereby suppressing the memories of their abductions; they walk right through walls, and they levitate people out of their beds and up through their ceilings, essentially dematerializing physical objects with their minds. They take people, cars and all, from highways and urban roads. They impregnate women with specially designed embryos and then harvest the fetuses after a few weeks, apparently to create hybrid species that are half-human and half-alien. They track their "subjects" by the use of miniature implants placed in various parts of their bodies. They follow bloodlines through many generations from great grandparents, grandparents, parents, aunts, uncles, siblings and children.

And if that isn't strange enough, they also recycle souls, a process we call reincarnation. This is not my idea of an alien. This describes something else—angelic or demonic entities, such as those described in the Bible and other ancient texts.

Over the many years since our first encounter in Australia, Strieber, Mack and I kept in touch and had gotten together whenever possible. I consider them good friends and probably the most interesting and intelligent people I have ever met. (It was a great loss to us and to UFO research when John Mack died in a car accident in 2004). Ever since that fateful night in 1986 when Strieber came face-to-face with that terrifying little creature we now refer to as a "Gray alien," Whitley and his now-deceased wife, Anne, devoted much of their time to learning more about this thing we call the "abduction" phenomenon. Their quest for answers is documented in a series of books: *Confirmation, Breakthrough, Transformation*, and *The Secret School*, as well as in constant updates on his internet website "Unknown Country" and his podcast, "Dreamland."

These activities happened in spite of the fact that he has had his name and reputation smeared by professional debunkers, close-minded skeptics, and the media in general. His detractors love to make fun of the fact that he described in detail his frightening experience of having a probe inserted into his rectum for the purpose of stimulating his prostate gland, causing him to ejaculate. For some reason, some in the media love to refer to the "anal probe" as something to laugh about and something peculiar only to Strieber. What they fail to mention is that this procedure is commonplace in the experiences of those men who have had the contact experience. Collecting sperm from men and ova from women, for the purpose of creating hybrid/alien babies, seems to be one of the main items on the alien agenda. (It is also likely that they somehow use human DNA to make bodies for themselves, due to their seeming inability to procreate on their own.)

All the trauma—the abductions—the medical procedures—the mind-bending knowledge he has been given—the unending ridicule in the press—— took a toll on his and Anne's psyches, as one can imagine. Even more hurtful was the reaction from their church. At a March 2023 lunch meeting at a cozy Italian restaurant near his home in Santa Monica, CA, Strieber explained to me what happened. "Anne loved to volunteer at the church. Whenever there was a need, she would be there to volunteer. But when they discovered who she was married to, they shunned her. They wouldn't have anything to do with her or with me." Yes, he is bitter, as well he should be, but he is equally resolute and determined to stay the course and to own the life he was given—a role that has helped perhaps millions of people around the world come to grips with their own experiences, allowing them to express their fears and concerns for the first time, and often testifying publicly about the reality of this bizarre phenomenon.

I have had the great honor to know Whitley and his lovely, late wife, Anne, and I can state firmly that they are/were of sound mind and extremely high intellect. I treasure the many times we have met in person to discuss our views on this extraordinarily strange phenomenon; there are few people who understand the deep implications for the entire human race implied by what the beings have revealed.

One of my most interesting visits with the Striebers was in early December 1996 when my wife and I travelled to San Antonio, Texas (where they were living at the time) to spend a day with them. That Sunday we all attended a Catholic Mass at Whitley's childhood church, St. Peter's Catholic Church. (Although I was raised first as a Catholic and later in life as a Presbyterian, I was no longer affiliated with a religious institution. But because my wife is a Catholic and we raised our three children in that faith, I attended Catholic Mass with my family for many years. Additionally, I still believe strongly in the teachings of Jesus Christ and particularly his secret teachings, which include the reality of reincarnation.) This visit coincided with the publication of Whitley's book, *The Secret School: Preparation for Contact,* (HarperCollins, 1997) which tells a very strange tale from his childhood in San Antonio.

After the Mass, Whitley was eager to show us his old neighborhood where some of his strangest experiences took place. He showed where his childhood home had once stood in the affluent Terrell Hills area. The quiet streets, lined with beautiful, majestic live-oak trees and expansive, well-manicured lawns gave us insights into Whitley's upper-class upbringing. He showed us the route he biked as a nine-year-old, through darkened streets on his way to midnight sessions at the "secret school" in the nearby woods. His recollections of those enigmatic lessons, led by a peculiar, hooded figure he had once assumed was a nun, always faded when he reached the the modest hut by the towering, broad-trunked live-oak tree. He only vaguely recalled some small benches that he and other neighborhood children would sit on as they were taught unknown lessons. Once, he got a peek under the woman's hood and was startled to see the face of something that looked like a "bug."

As an adult, he had searched for the strange live oak tree and the school, but had not been able to find them, although the woods located in the Olmos Basin were still nearly intact near the Incarnate Word University. But all that changed one day when he went to the woods with a film crew that asked to interview him in the area of his childhood memory. As he showed the film crew around, he suddenly noticed an old path amongst the trees leading diagonally up a steep hill. Half way up the hill, he found the old tree and the remnants of the secret school. The discovery shocked his memory, and soon he understood the truth behind the secret school.

As we got out of the car that Sunday afternoon in the parking lot of Incarnate Word and headed up the path into the woods, I wondered how a small boy would have had the courage to enter this dark and secluded area alone in the middle of the night, but I also knew how powerful the mind-control ability of the beings could be. The kids who attended those meetings must have been under their spell as well. I had investigated several cases in which children were taken from school playgrounds during recess, so this story was not difficult for me to believe.

We could see the main path was but a small trail, crowded on both sides by encroaching trees and vegetation. At night, I thought, it must be truly oppressive and frightening. Soon we discovered a faint, diagonal cut in the side of the hill, barely wide enough for one person. There was no doubt that at one time, a long time ago, it was used as a footpath by someone. This small trail leads to an astonishing tree that cannot be seen from the main path—a gnarled giant that looked as if it belonged in a fairy tale about dwarves and gnomes. Just ahead on the footpath, veering to the right, we discovered the remnants of an old wooden structure accompanied by what seemed to be small benches—marking the location of the secret school.

As we stood gazing at this evidence of a long-forgotten past, Whitley described the bizarre nature of the lessons he learned there as a child, and I wondered how the public would react to his memories of being taken through time and to other worlds and being shown frightening visions of a terrible future that awaited our planet—a future of wars and natural disasters, including droughts, huge wildfires, terrible storms, and food shortages. Such visions are commonly shown to experiencers as warnings about the damage we humans are inflicting upon the Earth and to all life on the planet. These lessons often include the mysteries of the human soul, the nature of death, and of reincarnation.

Later, we went to lunch at the San Antonio Country Club to discuss what we had just seen. We sat on the veranda, overlooking the lush golf course and ordered our food and drinks as if we had just finished a round of golf, and as if the world were just fine. It was a lovely day, and for a moment we chatted idly about our families and our everyday lives. But finally, I broke the reverie by asking Whitley to explain how he was able to continue being a Catholic after everything that had happened to him and all he had learned. He said, "Oh that's easy. When I became aware of the visitors, I was so terrified that I ran back to the Church." Clearly, Whitley saw the Church as a refuge from what he saw as the inherently evil nature of the beings who had destroyed his prosperous and peaceful life. Unfortunately, he later realized that his Church wanted nothing to do with him.

The Striebers had been devout Catholics, but over time, their devotion faded as they came to terms with the strange alien visitors. Breaking completely with Catholicism wasn't easy, though. He attended St. Anthony Elementary and then Central Catholic High. His family attended Sunday Mass at St. Peter's Catholic Church, where he was baptized and had his first communion. When facing a spiritual crisis, his instincts told him to seek sanctuary in the safest place he knew. However, rather than comforting them, the Church treated them as if they were possessed by demons. I have warned my subjects not to share their experiences with their ministers. Doing so hardly ever ends well. Inevitably, they are told they are dealing with the Devil, and they are told not to return to the congregation—the one place they had always leaned on for support.

3

Mack Attack

In April 1993, I found myself in a small commuter plane flying from Dallas to Fayetteville, AR, to attend my first UFO conference, and I felt grave misgivings. After all, I had a Ph.D. and had been a tenured associate professor of journalism and department chair at the University of Texas at El Paso from 1972-1982. I resigned my tenured position to go to work at the investment firm, Merrill Lynch, and I was now a vice-president and senior financial consultant, serving wealthy clients in West Texas, New Mexico and Mexico. "What would my clients think of me if they knew what I was doing?"

I thought to myself. "What would my company do if my boss found out I was attending a UFO conference in, of all places, Eureka Springs, AR?" And most importantly, I asked myself, "Why risk everything to spend four days surrounded by UFO nuts?" The only reason I could come up with for my sudden interest in the UFO mystery is that I felt compelled to go. Or maybe it was just insatiable curiosity—the kind that makes journalists take risks.

Of course, I didn't tell anyone at work where I was going; fortunately, as a top producer, I had the freedom to go and come as I pleased by just telling my assistant I was going to take a few days off. There was little chance anyone would find out. But still, I was nervous.

After landing at the small airport and picking up my checked bag, I looked around for the shuttle that was supposed to take me to the conference. As I scanned the parking area, I noticed a rickety-old station wagon and a guy with a long pony-tail holding up a sign that read "UFO" in big letters. He was wearing a Tee shirt with a drawing of a flying saucer on the front. It was the shuttle driver who would take four of us, all men, to the motel in Eureka Springs where the Ozark UFO Conference was held every year in April. I really didn't want to be seen getting into that vehicle, but there was no choice, so I nudged my way into the back seat, sitting next to two strangers; the third man was seated up front. We were now set for the hour-and-a-half drive through pig and chicken-farming country on a two-lane winding road in search of the *truth*. "Oh God, what did I get myself into?" I wondered.

I decided to strike up a conversation with the guys by asking simple questions like, "Where are you guys from?" and "Is this your first time attending the conference?" but the three attendees didn't seem interested in chit chat. Finally, after a long period of silence, one of them asked me a question, "Are you from the Bureau?"

I thought about the strange question for a few moments and then answered with a question, "Do you mean the Farm Bureau?"

"No," he responded sarcastically, "the Federal Bureau of Investigation, the FBI!"

"No, I'm not with the FBI! What would make you think that?"

"Well, most people who come to the conference aren't wearing dark-blue, pin-striped suits with button-down shirts and bright-red ties!"

And then it hit me. I hadn't had time to change when I left my office for the airport in El Paso, and I was not aware that people in the "UFO Community" were paranoid about government agents monitoring their every move. I tried to explain why I was dressed like an FBI agent, but to no avail. I couldn't get any conversation going, so I had to endure the long drive in absolute silence.

As soon as we arrived at the motel, I rushed into my room and changed into jeans and a non-descript shirt—nothing that could be considered "FBI-ish". Then I walked down to the convention center to register and to take a look at some of the UFO folks meandering around the vendor's tables, where all sorts of UFO-themed items were on sale. Already the crowds were gathering, even though the conference wouldn't start until the next morning. I spent some time standing back and judging the people, many of whom were already wearing their little gray-alien T-shirts and their stick-on name tags. I began to think I had made a big mistake. But then I glanced at the list of speakers that was in the packet they gave me when I registered, and something caught my attention: a professor of psychiatry from Harvard University would be giving a lecture on alien abductions; his name was Dr. John Mack. "What in the world would a professor of psychiatry from Harvard be doing at a place like this?" I wondered. I had never heard of him, but he would soon play a huge role in my life.

John Mack and Joe Lewels in an Australian rain forest in 1996. (Photo by Author)

When it came time for him to make his presentation, I took my seat at the back of the 400-seat auditorium. I wasn't going to get involved in any of these UFO groups, which had sprung up in cities all over America and beyond. I could see the speaker's podium clearly as a tall, lanky man with dark hair strode up casually to the podium. He was dressed in an open-collared shirt and slacks, and he was quite at home on the stage. He began speaking informally, without the aid of notes and his words took me completely by surprise—both shocking and entirely unforeseen. Dr. Mack came to the point quickly. After working with more than 100 abductees, he said, "I have not found any signs of mental disorders."

"What?" I thought. "Did I hear that correctly? Did a Harvard professor of psychiatry, who also happened to be a Pulitzer Prize winner, just say publicly, in front of video cameras at a UFO conference in Arkansas, that alien abductions were real?" He said it so casually, that it took a moment for his words to sink in, but the answer was, "Yes, he did!" He went on to explain that he had been asked by researcher Budd Hopkins to interview some of the abductees he had been working with. On a lark, Mack agreed. To say that Mack was skeptical about the whole UFO thing would be a gross understatement. He felt sure he would be able to resolve the mystery quickly. After all, he had been working as a clinical psychiatrist and as a full professor of psychiatry at Harvard for more than 30 years. If anyone could detect the slightest bit of hoaxing or delusions, it would be him. But he didn't. He was stunned at just how sane and credible the abductees were. There was no deception, only normal people who needed answers to their life-long involvement with mysterious, alien beings. Mack was hooked. He recognized immediately that he was facing a phenomenon that would turn the world of science upside down. Many people in his position would have gotten as far away from that world as possible. But Mack embraced it and began interviewing and working with abductees on an ongoing basis, even holding support-group meetings in his home.

Perhaps someone with strong religious beliefs or even an atheist would have been frightened off, but Mack was neither. He had been born to a secular, Jewish family. His parents were both intellectuals—college professors who raised their children to have open minds. Mack had already explored the effects of LSD and hallucinogenic plants on the human mind by trying them himself, and he had worked with famous LSD researcher, Dr. Stanislav Grof, trying to ascertain if such drugs had potential for therapeutic uses. Perhaps his lack of religious indoctrination as a child was a blessing, for it allowed him to seek extensively for answers regarding the greatest mysteries that we humans face. By the time he interviewed his first abductee, he had shown his fearlessness in pursuing controversial phenomena and following the data, wherever it led.

I remember that day in Arkansas clearly some 30 years later. Something happened to me while I was listening to Mack tell his story about meeting with abductees that is hard to explain. First, his presence at the conference totally knocked that chip off my shoulder; it was as if I had been shot by an invisible lightning bolt, and I knew with certainty that this UFO business was serious business. There were real, serious-minded people in high positions who were getting involved. Mack's credentials were so solid and his conclusions so straight forward that he single-handedly changed the paradigm of UFO research and our scientific understanding of the nature of reality.

Something else happened in that moment. Somehow, I knew I had to do something to support this courageous, and obviously brilliant, academician. I didn't realize it at the time, but I had found my purpose in life. I had to get involved; I couldn't keep sitting on the sidelines as an armchair researcher. Furthermore, I knew instinctively he was headed for trouble. No university, particularly Harvard, would want to be associated with the topic of alien abductions. There would, no doubt, be repercussions for what he had done. Having been in academics myself, I understood only too well how institutions of "higher" learning were, in fact, narrow-minded and ultra-protective of their reputations. But I had no idea at that moment what I could do to help. The solution came to me two days later.

Before leaving the conference, I was engaged in conversation with Walt Andrus, director of the Mutual UFO Network (MUFON), an organization of UFO investigators with chapters in major cities in the U.S. and abroad. It was known for using scientific methods to study the UFO phenomena and for debunking cases that didn't measure up to its strict standards. That organization had the credibility I needed to become a researcher. While speaking to Andrus, he suggested that I start a chapter in El Paso, and I agreed. That aura of credibility gave me an opportunity to get to the bottom of this bizarre mystery and find the answers for myself. If my findings supported Mack's conclusions, that would be helpful to him, but if they didn't, I would speak out and say so. I promised myself to keep an open mind and report the facts as I found them.

The story of how I organized a team, which included a psychiatrist and several certified hypnotherapists, is told at length in my book, *The God Hypothesis*, so I won't go into the details here; I will simply say we followed strict protocols to screen the experiencers who came to us for help, ensuring we were not being hoaxed, or we were not dealing with the mentally unbalanced. My three-year study led to my book and made me a sought-after speaker at New Age and UFO conferences in the U.S., Australia, and Mexico. That is how, in 1996, Dr. John Mack, Whitley Strieber, and I began life-long friendships when we were invited to speak at the Queensland International UFO Symposium.

We firmly believed that these so-called aliens were interdimensional beings who had always existed here. In contrast, researcher Budd Hopkins (1931-2011) and history professor David Jacobs argued that aliens came from other planets across the galaxy when humans discovered atomic power, a coincidence we found too convenient. The three of us stood solidly in the camp of those who believed these "so-called" aliens were not aliens at all, but interdimensional beings who had always been here.

The other, and more important part of the debate was the matter of the spiritual experiences reported by many abductees. John, Whitley and I believed this was the most important aspect of the phenomenon, but the other side pushed the idea that the aliens were evil and there was no spiritual growth involved. For them, the UFO mystery was simply understood as physical beings from other planets, coming to Planet Earth in physical spaceships and kidnapping humans for nefarious, covert experiments. The rift, which should have been a gentlemanly, scholarly debate, turned into an onslaught of verbal attacks by the materialists against those of us who saw a deeper meaning in the abduction experience.

In his second book on the subject, *Passport to the Cosmos*, Mack addressed the issue in his professorial way:

A dimension "of the abduction phenomenon might variously be defined as consciousness expanding, growth engendering, or spiritual. One of the most intense debates in this field occurs around the question of whether these changes in the psyche of the experiencers—no researchers seem to deny that such change, even transformation, does in fact occur in some cases—or is instead a kind of by-product, reflecting human creativity, resilience and adaptability in the face of traumatic challenge, or is even the result of alien trickery or deception.

"There is much confusion in the abduction research field surrounding the word *spiritual*. How, some argue, can a phenomenon that is so traumatic for many people, one that seems to disregard human wishes, feelings, and morality, be spiritual and emanating from a higher source? Some experiencers are left with external and possibly internal organ scarring, as well as lasting conscious and unconscious fears and phobias. Should not spiritual experiences be benign, largely uplifting, or enlightening? Yet we know that some experiences, such as life-threatening illnesses, tragic losses, and other personal crises, are often catalysts for profound personal growth and transformation.... Some abduction experiencers describe openings and connections to what they variously describe as the other world, Divine Light, Home, Source, or God."

"The expansion of psychic or intuitive abilities, a heightened reverence for nature with a the feeling of having a life-preserving mission, the collapse of space/time perception, a sense of entering other dimensions of reality or universes, the conviction of possessing a dual human/alien identity, a feeling of connection with all of creation, and related transpersonal experiences—all are such frequent features of the abduction phenomenon that I have come to feel that they are, at least potentially, basic elements of the process."

Mack continues, "Even when abductees initially experience the beings themselves, especially the now well-known gray figures with huge black eyes, as instigators of great fear and trauma, over time they may come to see them as odd spirit guides, closer to the ultimate creative principle or Source than humans, even as emissaries from the Divine. Abductees also commonly experience a poignant sense that they have themselves become too separated from Home, Source, or God, and will cry and rage against the fact that they have been incarnated or reincarnated back on Earth... and they have made some sort of agreement with the beings or the Creator itself to fulfill a human mission." (Pp. 17-18)

The response from the Hopkins/Jacobs duo to this way of thinking was not a reasonable or gentlemanly one. They jointly went on the attack, asserting that Mack and other researchers simply didn't know how to investigate abduction cases or perform hypnosis properly. They claimed they alone could detect what they termed "confabulation" (fantasy) by their research subjects while under hypnosis. It wasn't that their subjects were not reporting such things, it was simply that any such information reported to them—information that did not conform to their materialistic/atheistic view of the world—particularly if it smacked of the spiritual or transformative—was simply discarded as fantasy and never reported in their books or lectures. Additionally, they were making unethical suggestions to their subjects while under hypnosis, suggesting the beings were evil and should not be doing the hurtful medical procedures accompanying the abductions. Interestingly, neither Hopkins nor Jacobs were certified hypnotherapists, nor did they operate under the supervision of a psychiatrist. In fact, they were not therapists at all. They were just hypnotists who did not feel it necessary to follow the code of ethics used by certifying institutions and by MUFON. From 1993-2000, I served as a consultant and assistant director for West Texas and Southern New Mexico for that organization. In defense of Mack, I wrote an article for the May, 1998, issue of the *MUFON Journal*, after the publication of Jacobs's book, *The Threat.*

"David Jacobs has thrown down the gauntlet to most other abduction researchers in his current book, *The Threat,* and he has unfairly singled out perhaps the most prestigious member of the research community, Dr. John Mack, for a special scolding.... Those who do not meet his personal standards of research, or who don't agree with his interpretation of the facts, are 'incompetent, New Age Positives, who band together into almost cult-like groups.' In Jacobs's view, these researchers have turned UFO research into a religion and have seriously strayed from accepted scientific standards. The result, in his view, is that they have wrongly reached the conclusion that alien abductions are not so bad, and, in some cases, they can even be positive. He, on the other hand, due to his 'correct' methodology, knows the real truth—that alien hybrids are secretly plotting to take over the Earth, and, due to their superior intellect, usurp control from their human counterparts.... He cannot accept that there are out-of-body experiences, past-life memories, or other paranormal phenomena that have yet to be explained or accounted for by mainstream researchers. Such notions, in his view, are simply 'New-Age foolishness' that do not merit serious thought."

There were others who found Mack's work with abductees, and the media blitz of ridicule and skepticism that accompanied his 1994 book, *Abduction: Human Encounters with Aliens*, an embarrassment. These were Mack's colleagues in the department of psychiatry at Harvard University, who were feeling impacted by the world-wide attention the book received. As I had predicted when I first heard him speak at the conference in Arkansas, Dr. Mack faced a legal attack from his peers at Harvard who formed an *ad hoc* committee to investigate Mack's methodology; their goal was to have him fired, have his tenure removed, and possibly have his medical license removed as well. The legal battle cost him more than $100,000 in legal fees and damaged his reputation even further. But after more than a year of incredible stress, Mack finally won his case by citing academic freedom and by gathering the support of dozens of psychologists and academics from all over the country. I was honored to have been one of the many who wrote letters in support of Mack's cause, in an effort to convince the committee that Mack's work and conclusions were not only valid, but essential to the true understanding of the nature of reality.

Over the years since our meeting in Australia, John and I kept in touch by phone, email, and by meeting in person at conferences where we were both speaking. He asked me to accompany him to Mexico to conduct research and meet with many experiencers in Mexico City and environs. I invited him to El Paso to speak at a public meeting that I had arranged, and I met with him, Whitley Strieber, Apollo astronaut Edgar Mitchell, and billionaire Lawrence Rockefeller at a small, private retreat in SC. Over the years, until his death in London in 2004, John and I were collaborating on projects and confiding in each other about our deepest concerns involving the abduction mystery. "I don't think they're aliens," he told me early on in his research. "They are much closer to the Divine than humans are."

"Yes," I agreed. "I think they are of the angelic realm."

At the time of his tragic death, John and I were co-authoring a presentation and paper regarding a species of beings who had been turning up in our research, but which he had previously been reluctant to address in his books. We called it "The Reptilian Project." After his death, researcher Barbara Lamb and I carried on with the project and presented our findings at a 2005 UFO conference in Laughlin, NV. But it just wasn't the same without the gravitas he would have lent the lecture. He is sorely missed for his open-minded approach to science and his willingness to courageously go wherever the data led him, even at the risk of his stellar career. I treasure the words he inscribed in my copy of his book, *Abduction: Human Encounters with Aliens*: "To Joe, whose pioneering work will, I believe, lead us in time, to realize the Divine Source of this extraordinary phenomenon. With thanks and much appreciation, warmly, John." To this, I can only say, "Thank you, John, for helping me find my purpose in life."

Author's note: For more information about Dr. Mack's life, read Ralph Blumenthal's 2022 book, *The Believer*. (High Road Books, University of New Mexico Press) Although this book provides a look into Mack's private life, it incorrectly brands him as a "believer." John was not a "believer," he was a "knower." The first is based on faith and the second is based on knowledge, and John was undoubtedly a man of knowledge.

4

Healing Wounds, Finding Purpose

I have had many cases in which my subjects spontaneously recalled past-life memories while under hypnosis. Many recall such memories without hypnosis, so I know hypnosis itself is not responsible for such memories. I am also certain that hypnotic subjects are not being influenced by the therapist who could be introducing the idea of a particular time period or past life with subtle suggestions. In fact, I found, during my almost 30 years as a certified hypnotherapist, people in a trance do not accept misleading suggestions, but rather they push back by correcting the therapist when a leading question is asked.

One way to make sure the person is not prone to accept misleading suggestions is to intentionally attempt to mislead the subject. These tests are designed to weed out anyone who is highly suggestible or is making up his story intentionally. For example, if the person is remembering being placed on a table on a spacecraft by alien beings, for the purpose of performing medical procedures, I might ask "please describe the table and its four legs." The response is always the same: "I don't see four legs. There is just one big pedestal in the middle." Such an answer conforms to the descriptions other experiencers have given regarding the tables they have seen. Sometimes I would ask the subject to look at the corners of the room to see if there is anything of interest there. The answer was always like this: "There are no corners" or, "I don't see any corners; the room is round." Such questions are both logical and leading at the same time. Most tables we have on Earth have four legs, and most rooms have corners. Yet that is never the case in the crafts. This technique is a good way to test the subject's veracity and suggestibility; I always throw in such questions in the course of a hypnotic regression. There are other questions pertaining to more obscure features of the beings and of their procedures that I will not go into here.

Another reason to accept that hypnosis, in the hands of a qualified and certified therapist, elicits true memories is the fact that the therapy very often has a healing effect. It cures irrational phobias and provides answers to questions the person has had about his/her life. Additionally, the subject often has strong emotional responses regarding past-life memories of persons they loved or detested in the past, or of traumatic experiences. A good example is the case of a 41-year-old woman who came to me for help because of a debilitating case of claustrophobia. Even though she was a psychotherapist, she could not figure out why she was having panic attacks.

She called me with a discernible touch of panic in her voice: "A friend of mine told me you're a hypnotherapist, and I'm hoping you can help me. I don't know who else to turn to. I'm at my wit's end."

"I'll be happy to try, just tell me more about it," I responded.

"Well," she continued, "during a flight coming back to El Paso from a trip to India, I was suddenly gripped with such terror of being enclosed in a small space (she was flying coach) that I rushed to the door and tried to open it. A flight attendant grabbed me and forced me into a seat, then she made me drink two of those little bottles of scotch. This finally calmed me down. I have no idea why I did that, and now I'm afraid to fly."

After she described this event to me, I agreed to try to help her. At a subsequent meeting, I put her into a trance state and began to speak to her subconscious mind to find the root cause of her problem. (Psychiatrists agree that healing can only take place when the root cause of the problem is discovered. In traditional therapy this is done over a series of sessions that can last months or even years.)

Once she was in a trance, I simply suggested "Just go to the very first time you ever felt this way." Immediately the woman began coughing and choking; she was unable to speak and couldn't answer my questions regarding what was happening. So I said, "Just move forward in time to the point when you are able to speak."

"I'm dead. I've left my body. I'm home again. All my friends are here and they are surrounding me and laughing. It's like a reunion."

I said, "Go back and look at what happened to you."

"They were burying me alive!" she cried, with tears in her eyes and anger in her voice.

"Who?" I asked.

"The Catholic Church. They said I was a heretic."

In the debriefing, she explained that she had been chained to a wall with another person at her side. They were in a dungeon or basement of a church or monastery, and the killers had been sealing up the niche with bricks. The last bricks were placed just inches in front of their faces, suffocating them to death—a horrible death indeed, and one that could certainly be the cause of her present problem. But before ending the session, I had her look at the scene once more and see that the people who did that to her were to be pitied because they were not spiritually evolved souls. Then I asked her if she could find it in her heart to forgive them. And with a deep breath and tears in her eyes, she said that she could.

"Well," she said afterward, with great relief, "That explains the panic attacks, and it explains why I am so against the Catholic Church and against Jesus. But here is the strangest thing; when I was on the other side, I heard the voice of Jesus. He said, 'Don't judge me by what others have done in my name.' He's right. I have blamed him for what the Church has done in his name. But I won't anymore."

The hypnosis session lasted no more than one hour, but she came away a changed person. The claustrophobia was gone. She never had another panic attack, and she was able to board airplanes stress free. She was still against the Catholic Church, but she stopped blaming Jesus for what the Church had done. Furthermore, without any suggestions from me, she discovered with certainty that she had lived before, that she was more than just her body, and that death is merely an illusion. Most importantly, she lost her fear of death. That one-hour hypnosis session was a life-changing experience for her and a testament to the validity of hypnosis. I doubt traditional psychotherapy would have ever been able to help her.

Another case is that of a 33-year-old woman who traveled from Sydney, Australia, to Laughlin, NV, in March, 2000, to ask me to help her deal with a lifetime of terrifying abduction experiences. She had read online that I would be one of the speakers at a large, international UFO conference, and she decided to work up the courage to undergo hypnosis.

It turned out I remembered her from my time in Australia when I was a speaker once again at the second UFO conference in Brisbane. She had bought a copy of *The God Hypothesis* and had attended my lecture. She felt I was the only one she could trust with her delicate problem. She approached me the evening before the start of the proceedings and asked me if I might have time during the week-long conference to help her come to terms with her life-long abductions at the hands of what she believed to be evil beings. I noticed she was very thin and had a dour expression on her face—a sign of years of stress.

After the initial interview, where she made her case, I decided that she would make a good candidate for hypnosis. Although she seemed very nervous and appeared to be suffering from depression, she still met my requirements for the procedure. She seemed very intelligent and well-spoken. She made her case clearly and concisely, and she had traveled more than 8,000 miles just to meet with me. It was clear that she needed help; she felt this was her only chance to confront her demons.

She began by telling me about her life as the child of a broken home who had difficulty relating to her parents and most others. Although she was raised in a Christian church, she had renounced her faith, and as a teenager she had begun to "tune out the world by living a life of sex, drugs and rock and roll." She explained that she was pissed off at Jesus and her folks for not protecting her from the evil creatures that had harassed her since she was a small child. She had lost all faith in God and in the people around her.

"I just wanted to tune out the world, so I started drinking and smoking pot in high school and then dropping out. I haven't been able to have any long-lasting relationships with men. As soon as they start getting serious, I just dump them. I just feel like I don't belong here on planet earth—like I was just dumped here. Nothing about my life makes sense. And then there's the creatures that have been terrifying me since I was a child," she said.

"I have had vivid dreams, or at least I call them dreams, of being taken on a craft and being placed on a metal table with someone putting a long needle into the side of my head. I've always had a fear of the dark, and even now I have to sleep with a light on or the TV on. Sometimes at night I wake up and I'm paralyzed. I can't move or scream, but there is someone in the room next to my bed. It just goes on and on. I've never felt connected to this world; I've never felt a sense of belonging or a sense of purpose."

She seemed to me to be totally worn out from trying to distance herself from the aliens. I explained to her that what she was doing took a lot of energy. "No wonder you're exhausted," I told her. "It's as if you're going through life holding a basketball underwater and trying to keep it there for fear of what you might learn if it pops up." She laughed and admitted that was exactly how she felt.

The following afternoon we met to conduct the hypnosis session, and after 20 minutes or so, she was able to reach a deep trance state. Soon, I took her to the time when she was on that inevitable metal table on the craft, and the reality of the experience set in. It was no dream. Her breathing became rapid—her heart racing. These are the signs of high stress and fear. Instead of letting her relive the pain and anguish in its entirety, I used a technique I developed; I suggested that she could view the scene from above, as if she were out of her body. "Just look at it from above and see it objectively, without the pain and fear. Just look down and report to me calmly what you see happening as if you're watching it on a TV screen." (It always amazes me how well this works.) She was able to take a deep breath and calm down and begin describing the scene below. "Oh, there are three creatures surrounding the table. One of them is putting this long needle into my head."

"What do they look like?" I asked. "Can you describe them?"

"They have big black eyes. They're small and skinny and they have big heads."

"What color is their hair?" I asked, trying to lead her astray. It was one of my leading questions designed to see if she was suggestible.

"No, they don't have hair. They're bald."

"OK, then, I want you to look carefully at them and ask yourself if they are intentionally trying to hurt you."

"No, they're not trying to hurt me."

"Oh that's good to know. Are they trying to frighten you?"

"No, they're not trying to frighten me."

"Oh, that's also good to know. They aren't trying to hurt you, and they aren't trying to frighten you. That's great. Now try to decide if they are evil."

(Long pause). "No, I don't think they're evil. I can't believe I'm saying this, but they aren't evil!" she said excitedly.

"That's great. They aren't trying to hurt you or frighten you and they aren't evil. That's wonderful! You'll have to remember that. Now there is one more question: Why of all the billions of people on this planet are you the one lying on that table?"

"It's my purpose," she responded tearfully. "I had a choice. I could go to Earth and have children and have a normal life, or I could do this. I chose this life. I volunteered! I never volunteer for anything!"

"I don't understand," I said, feigning ignorance. "Why would you choose this difficult life rather than a normal life? That doesn't make sense."

"It's like...it's like getting more brownie points on my karma board. It's for the greater good," she explained. "If I chose this life I would get credit for five lifetimes. I was so excited about doing it. I was so looking forward to it. It was like a firm handshake—a deal. It was solid! But I forgot. The plan was for me to be part of the breeding program."

The breeding program, she explained in the post-hypnosis debriefing, involved allowing herself to be impregnated by the beings with embryos that would produce hybrid children, which they showed her many times when she was aboard their craft. The fetuses would be harvested a few weeks later. "I saw the fetuses in tanks of liquid being grown until they were ready to come out," she said. "Then they showed me my children. They looked frail and ill, with patchy hair like cancer patients. It frightened me, and I felt so sorry for them. The beings are creating a new species of humans who will do a better job of taking care of the planet. It's for the greater good."

"Let's be clear about when you volunteered for this program. When did that happen?"

"It was between lives, when I was planning my next life. I didn't have a body; I was just like a spark."

"Who gave you the choice?"

"God, and the beings on the craft. We were all in spirit form—no bodies. Now everything makes sense. My life makes sense for the first time. I've had such a bad attitude toward religion and particularly Jesus, but now I see I wasn't abandoned. I really misjudged him. Now I can let him back into my heart. I think now I can be a better person and lead a more normal life. It makes such a difference knowing I'm not a victim. I'm going to stop taking drugs and drinking alcohol. I might even be able to find someone that I can actually have a relationship with. Maybe even children. Now I know why I never wanted a serious relationship. It would have led to having children, and I didn't want children because they scared me. Now I know why."

The difference in her appearance and attitude after the hypnosis was amazing. No longer dour and stressed, she was now bubbly and smiling. In fact, she couldn't stop smiling. She learned so much during the session—that Jesus hadn't abandoned her, that she had lived before, and that she would live again. Most importantly, she learned that she wasn't just a body made of flesh and bones, but rather an immortal, spiritual being. She also learned that her "tormentors" were not evil, but, in fact, had been with her between lives to help her plan her next life on Earth. She need not be in a constant state of fear, and she could start living a normal life. Remembering the hybrid children was difficult and it would take time to process those memories, but, in all, the hypnosis was a great success—she returned to Australia, a changed and happy person.

In all the years I have used the technique of asking why they, of all the people on Earth, are the ones being "abducted," I have never had anyone say that the beings are evil, and they always say that they made an agreement to play the role of abductee in their new life. Yes, souls have some choices about their next life, but they never get the choice to *not* reincarnate. That is mandatory. There are lessons that must be learned, and there are wrongs that must be righted. The in-between life is where we learn about pre-destination and missions that must be carried out. Our lives on Earth have a purpose, even if it doesn't seem like it when we live them.

Chapter 5

The Cosmic Coffee Table

There are many other examples of cases I have worked on in which the subject has described the in-between life, but perhaps none as aptly as the 33-year-old woman named Melanie, who came to me with vague memories of "being harvested" by aliens. She spoke with a bit of a Texas drawl, having been raised in Lubbock, TX, where she had led a poor and deprived childhood. Yet she had a good sense of humor and seemed cheerful most of the time. She explained that she always wanted to be a healer, so she became a Registered Nurse, but later turned to massage therapy so she could use her hands to heal her patients. She believed she had been given the power to heal with energy that radiated through her hands.

The following week, when we began a series of hypnosis sessions, she appeared determined, but nervous, to uncover hidden memories. Her fears were confirmed when she found herself on an operating table in a spaceship surrounded by frightening creatures that included reptilian beings. Once again, I suggested that she look at the scene from above as if she were floating out of her body and looking at the scene objectively. When I asked her why they chose her to abduct, she immediately said, "I volunteered."

"Go to that place and time when you volunteered," I suggested.

Pausing, she said, "It's like I'm sitting around a cosmic coffee table with higher beings and the souls of those who agree to play their roles in our next lives. We don't have physical bodies; we're just sparks of light. We agree to be born at certain times, in certain places, and to find each other on Earth at the appointed time. Then we can carry out the plans we agreed to at that coffee-table meeting."

But then we forget. Our conscious memories of those agreements are erased as we are born into new bodies, but yet our subconscious, or as I prefer to think of it, our "higher" consciousness has access to those memories through meditative states such as hypnosis.

A Gray escorting a soul into the light.

(Courtesy of Janet Bergmark,
author of In the Presence of Aliens)

But, what is the point of making those detailed plans if we are to forget them when we are born again as a human? For that, there can only be one answer. Life on Earth is a test. If we already knew the answers, what would be the point? As humans we have choices to make and lessons to learn. The opportunities to learn are planned for us before we are born. Often, those lessons are harsh and painful. Will we do the right thing and forgive our enemies, or will we carry a grudge and seek revenge? Will we carry through with our promise to love and care for someone "till death do us part?" Or will we abandon that person when the going gets rough? Will we find ways to serve others, or will we choose the selfish route? Will we eschew material wealth, or will we get caught up in a life of luxury? The choices we make will determine whether or not we will have to come back again and again, to be born of a woman and suffer the struggles of being chained once more to a human body.

In regressive hypnotherapy, it is important to ask the person who is remembering a past life to go to the final day of that lifetime and to experience their death. This may seem cruel, but It is at this crucial moment that the subject remembers the vows he or she made, the lessons learned, and the mistakes made in that life. In the case of Melanie, who remembered being at a "cosmic coffee table," she had just remembered a past life in London in the early 1700s. She was married to a doctor but was disappointed that she couldn't be a doctor herself. Instead, she had to play the traditional role of supportive housewife and mother. She also remembered being an abductee in that life.

On her deathbed on the last day of her life, she was surrounded by her servants; her loving husband had died before her and she wept as she remembered how much she loved him. As she left her body I asked her what she learned from that lifetime and she said, "I wanted to achieve more than just being a housewife; I wanted to be a healer."

In her current life she was able to be a healer as a nurse and as a massage therapist. The gray aliens helped her by sending their energy through her as she worked on her patients.

On the last day of that life, her spirit left her body and began to move toward the light; she said with great surprise, "Oh, the wee ones are here!"

"Who are the wee ones?" I asked.

"They're the Grays. They take me into the light. They're always with me. They're my guides."

On more than one occasion my subjects remembered more than one lifetime in one session. A forty-five year-old man who worked in the financial services industry, remembered a troubling life two thousand years ago. He found himself riding a white horse and wearing leather boots that laced up his calf with leather straps. "Who are you in that life?" I asked.

"I'm a Roman soldier."

"Where are you?"

"Jerusalem."

"Where are you going?"

"I'm leaving. I don't want to be here anymore," he said with tears in his eyes.

"What's happening?"

"They're crucifying criminals. I've seen many executions. There's trouble in the city. There are Jews stirring up trouble and killing Roman soldiers and tax collectors. They're assassins who deserve to be beaten and crucified as examples of what happens to the trouble makers. But the one who was crucified today was not a criminal. He was a holy man who never did anything wrong. I have to get away; I don't want to do this anymore," he said, with tears running down his cheeks.

"Did you know him?"

"I heard him speak to a crowd. He spoke about loving your enemies. He was a healer, not a trouble maker."

"What was the man's name?"

"I don't know. He was a Jewish holy man."

"Is this the man we know as Jesus today?"

"Yes," he replied as he sobbed uncontrollably.

"What did you learn from that life?" I asked, as he relived the last day of his life as a Roman soldier. "I will never follow orders blindly. I don't want to be a soldier again."

Not wanting to leave him in that sad state of mind, I suggested he go back to the first time he incarnated on Earth. He found himself in the body of a man wearing animal skins for clothes and carrying a large axe for protection.

"I live in a cave," he said. "There aren't many people on Earth. I'm searching for game, but I have to be careful; there are dangerous bears and big-toothed cats. My clan members are all dead. I'm alone. It's a hard life."

"Go to the last day of your life," I suggest.

"I died alone in my cave. I had no one else in my life."

"And what did you learn in that life that you brought with you into this life?"

"I don't want to be alone anymore. I want a wife and family. I don't want to die alone again."

"OK," I suggested, "now go forward in time. What happens next?"

"I've died. I'm going home."

Invariably, the soul is given a life review, which some might call a moment of judgment. He is shown the actions he took and the decisions he made that either hurt others or were acts of kindness. It's time to learn those things he needs to work on in his next life. There is a period of rest and reunion with old friends, but eventually a new life on Earth is planned and new parents are chosen. Back to Earth again.

Section II

Ancient Connections

6

The River Lethe

How far back in history did humans begin to understand the concepts of karma and reincarnation? (The word reincarnation derives from the Latin, meaning "entering into the flesh again.") No one knows for sure, but it's likely that people have always known. Certainly, in India and Asia the religions of Buddhism and Hinduism were based on the teaching of the cycles of birth, life, death and rebirth in ancient times. In the Western world the concept appears in ancient Greek mythology. For example, it was believed the soul had to pass through the underworld on its journey in the afterlife. There, the River Lethe was one of the five rivers of Hades. The word Lethe means "forgetfulness" or "oblivion." The River Lethe was said to flow around the cave of Hypnos (the god of sleep) and through the underworld where all those who drank from it experienced complete forgetfulness.

The souls of the dead were believed to be required to drink the waters of the Lethe in order to forget their Earthly lives; it was only when their memories were erased that they would be reincarnated.

But there was hope. The god Orpheus would give some souls a password, allowing them to drink from the pool of memory (Mnemosyne) instead. This act would restore their memories of their past lives. An Orphic inscription, dated from between the second and third century BC, warned readers to avoid the Lethe and to seek the Mnemosyne instead, to avoid having their memories erased.

In ancient Greek tradition, Lethe was also thought of as a goddess, much like the goddess Meng Po of Chinese mythology, who would wait on the Bridge of Forgetfulness to serve the souls of the dead a soup that would erase their memories before they could be reincarnated.

Were the stories of reincarnation in ancient Greek and Chinese mythology simply fairy tales, or were there those who took the ideas seriously? One only need turn to the writings of the Greek poet Pindar (518-438 BC) and philosopher and physician, Empedocles (494-434 BC) to see that belief in reincarnation was indeed taken seriously. Both believed in the concept of karma and that the soul is immortal, pre-existent and divine. Such ideas were promoted by Pythagoras who, it is said, once told a man who was beating a dog to stop because the dog had the soul of his deceased friend.

Bust of Plato

Plato (428-348 BC), perhaps the most influential philosopher of the ancient world, wrote that the soul goes through repeated incarnations until it is able to quell its desire of material possessions and return to its original state in the invisible world. Plato's *The Republic*, his most famous philosophical work, taught in institutions of higher learning throughout the world, promotes reincarnation:

"Now when all the souls had chosen their lives...they all traveled into the plain of Lethe... In the evening they encamped by the Forgetful River, whose water no pitcher can hold. And all were compelled to drink a certain measure of its water, and those who had no wisdom to save them, drank more than the measure. And as each man drank, he forgot everything." (Plato, *The Republic*, Book X)

Plato describes the case of Er, the Chaldean, who had a near-death experience in which he witnessed the souls of the dead choosing their next lives and forgetting the lives they just lived. Plato's influence extended far into the future, and was embraced by early Christian leaders such as Origen, Basiledes and others whose writings were later declared heretical by the Orthodox Church.

But where did these Greek ideas about the soul originate? Many believe there was actually a prophet in ancient Greece named Orpheus, who first introduced this theology and inspired these writers and philosophers. Orpheus is said to have founded a mysterious sect called the "Orphici" in ancient Thrace, which taught that the soul is divine, immortal, and aspires to freedom, while the body holds it in fetters as a prisoner. Death, he taught, releases the soul temporarily, but then it is re-imprisoned after a short time. Over time, the story of Orpheus was relegated to the genre of mythology, and stories of his exploits were the subject of fanciful tales in which it is said he traveled to the underworld to retrieve the soul of his dead wife, Eurydice.

Early Christian scholar Origen (185-253 AD) wrote in his book, *De Principiis*: "Every soul comes into this world strengthened by the victories or weakened by the defeats of its previous life. Its place in this world as a vessel appointed to honor or dishonor is determined by its previous merits or demerits. Its work in this world determines its place in the world which is to follow this..."

Hinduism and Buddhism are both founded on the concept of the transmigration of the soul and mirror the concepts found in Greek theology. Hinduism taught that the soul is in an endless cycle of reincarnation with no end, while Buddhism taught that the cycle would end when enlightenment (Nirvana) was achieved. Once a soul lived a perfect life—embracing poverty, devoting itself to the service of others and loving all things unconditionally, it could bypass the trap of reincarnation and enter a place of eternal bliss. These teachings go as far back as the first millennium BC and can be found in the Sanskrit texts known as the Vedas, originating in ancient India, such as the Mahabharata, the Bhagavada Purana, and the Bhagavad Gita, among others.

Buddhists believe that to live is to suffer (see Chapter 28), and to die is to be released from suffering, only to be born again as a human and suffer once more. The cycle of life and death and reincarnation, is known as Samsara, the inexorable turning of the wheel of karma, forcing souls to return to Earth endlessly. Release, it was believed, comes only through enlightenment—the compassionate awareness of the universal oneness of all things. In Buddhist teachings, enlightenment is the door to Nirvana, an escape from the wheel to the non-physical realm. The teachings hold that suffering comes from the ego's self-awareness, its illusion of a distinction between self and other. The Buddha taught that each individual soul determined its own fate by creating, with deeds and thoughts, the karmic ledger governing progress toward enlightenment.

In its more than 2,500 year history, Buddhism spread from India to the Asian continent. Clearly, the knowledge of reincarnation was wide-spread in the ancient world, not only because many people remembered past lives, just as many do today, but also because enlightened beings such as Krishna, Buddha and Jesus taught the concept to their followers. Knowledge of life after death and rebirth has also been known as a result of cases of people who have had near-death experiences, (much like Plato's story of Er, the Chaldean) and those who return to the material world with detailed descriptions of what the afterlife is like. (See also Theosophy, Kabbalah, The Druze and Rosicrucian teachings as other examples.)

7

The Essenes

The first-century Jewish historian Josephus (37-100 AD) in his *Antiquity of the Jews*, book 18, says there were three sects of philosophy among the Jews: the Pharisees, the Sadducees, and the Essenes. The Sadducees, he said, believe that the soul dies with the body, but both the Pharisees and the Essenes believed in the rebirth of the soul after the death of the body. "The Essenes," he adds, "believed that the bodies were corruptible, but the souls are immortal and continue forever. But when the soul re-enters a body, it is like a prison. When the soul is set free from the bonds of the flesh, it rejoices. The Essenes shun pleasures as a vice and regard temperance and control of the passions as a special virtue.... They have a law that new members on admission to the sect shall forfeit their property to the order, with the result that you will nowhere see either abject poverty or inordinate wealth.... The war with the Romans tried their souls through and through by every variety of test. Racked and twisted, burnt and broken, and made to pass through every instrument of torture in order to induce them to blaspheme their lawgiver or to eat some forbidden thing, never once did they cringe to their persecutors or shed a tear." (The Jewish War 2.119-154.)

These, of course, were the keepers of the sacred scrolls found near the shores of the Dead Sea in 1947.

Thanks to the writings of Josephus and the amazing discovery of the ancient scrolls in caves near the ruins of the Essene community, now known as Qumran, we know a great deal about this mysterious Jewish sect that lived in isolation, practicing their own, ascetic brand of Judaism.

We now know the ancient Jews commonly believed their great prophets were the reincarnations of previous prophets. Moses, they believed, was the reincarnation of Abel, the son of Adam. Many Jews who wished fervently to be freed from the oppression of Roman rule believed a messiah would be the reincarnation of Adam, who had already been born as David, the third king of the united kingdom of Israel, and lived in approximately 1,000 BC. This messiah was to be a great warrior who would liberate the Jews from their Roman oppressors.

However, according to Dead Sea Scrolls scholar John Allegro, in *The Dead Sea Scrolls and the Christian Myth,* the Essenes believed that the Messiah would be the reincarnation of the patriarch Joshua, who led the Jews into the Promised Land after the death of Moses. Although the scrolls do not mention the Essene leaders by name, but rather by title, Allegro believed their leader, known as "The Teacher of Righteousness," was in fact the reincarnated Joshua. His proper name, "Joshua", is translated into Greek of the New Testament as "Jesus," and in ancient Hebrew, it would be "Yeshua of Yoshua."

Although Allegro's claims are disputed by the other Scroll scholars, his discovery would explain an enigma that has haunted Bible scholars and Christians for two millennia. Why would the angel, Gabriel (Luke 1:31), tell the Virgin Mary that her child would be named "Jesus"?

"And the angel said unto her. 'Fear not, Mary, for thou hast found favor with God. And behold, thou shalt conceive in thy womb, and bring forth a son, and shalt call his name Jesus.'"

Why "Jesus"? There had to be a reason. The only explanation that makes sense is that the child would be the reincarnation of Joshua, and only the Essenes believed that this would be the case. The Dead Sea Scrolls make it clear that the Essenes were preparing a place for the messiah to be born—a place of purity, where he would be kept safe from the sinful influences of the outside world, and from his natural enemies, the Pharisees, who considered the Essenes competitors and heretics. In their well-founded paranoia, the Essenes chose to never refer to their members, leaders and enemies by name, but only by titles. Their community was a place of isolation on the shores of the Dead Sea, shrouded in secrecy and mystery—a place that would protect them from the Pharisees, who were appointed as heads of Herod's Temple by their Roman controllers, and who were

Hiding the sacred scrolls in the caves of Qumran

using the Temple as a means to enrich themselves, contrary to God's laws.

As obvious as this connection may seem to some scholars, the notion that the Jesus of the New Testament was actually the Essene Teacher of Righteousness is simply unacceptable to most Christians. Firstly, the concept of reincarnation is not part of modern-day theology, and secondly, the Scrolls have no mention of such things as a virgin birth, a crucifixion (although the Scrolls imply that their Teacher was persecuted and even murdered by his enemy, "The Wicked Priest.") Additionally, there is no mention of the raising of the dead, walking on water, or bodily resurrection. The Scrolls do not imply that their Teacher was God incarnate, and, importantly, there is no mention of a disciple who would inherit the right to act as his successor after his death. Such a notion is anathema to the Catholic Church, which is founded on the belief that the apostle, Peter, was named by Jesus to be his successor, and the belief that Catholic popes are Peter's successors.

How then, if Jesus was in fact the Teacher of Righteousness, did all these magical stories make it into the New Testament? And why are they written in Greek, rather than the ancient Hebrew language (Aramaic) that Jesus spoke? The obvious answer is that what we know as today's scriptures are believed to have been written 25 to 120 years after the life of Jesus. There was ample time for the legends to be exaggerated by overzealous followers. In fact, there are no original texts of the books of the New Testament, but only copies of copies of copies, written and changed by unknown hands. Yet, they are still held as absolute truths by the Orthodox Church. (See *Misquoting Jesus: The Story Behind Who Changed the Bible and Why*, by Bible scholar Bart Erhman.) In contrast, the Dead Sea Scrolls are written in ancient Hebrew, ancient Greek, and Aramaic, and they predate the earliest Gospels by at least 50 years. They are loosely dated to having been written between 120 BC and 68 AD (clearly during the time of Christ.) Their discovery by a Bedouin goat herder in 1947 was seen as a treasure trove of information about the origins of Christianity and early Judaism. Whatever they contained had the potential to either support today's version of Christianity, or explode any myths or exaggerations that may be contained in the Bible. For better or worse, they provided a peek into the world of Jesus never before available.

As they were slowly examined and translated, it became clear that the similarities between the Essenes and the earliest Christians, as described in the Scrolls are striking. Both Jesus and the Teacher presided over a council or group of 12 followers (disciples). Both the Essenes and the early Christians ate communal meals and practiced a form of baptism, which involved ritual bathing for the cleansing of sins. The members all took vows of poverty, giving up their possessions to the community. They worshiped at the temple together and ate their meals together.

"The Acts of the Apostles," says of the early Christians, "The faithful all owned everything in common." And, "They went as a body to the Temple each day." Both groups were known as healers, and both were at odds with the leaders of the Jerusalem Temple—the Pharisees. John Allegro (1923-1988), a British archaeologist and linguist was the only one of the original Scroll team members who was not a Catholic priest; his interpretation of the Scrolls differed greatly from that of the Catholic members of the team. He believed the information in the texts would undermine the whole basis of Christian beliefs. Allegro was educated at the University of Manchester and Oxford and was the only one of the select group of scholars who dutifully published those texts assigned to him. Raised as a Protestant, he became an agnostic as he understood the true implications of the ancient texts. He suggested that the Scrolls prove that the Biblical Jesus never existed, but rather was an amalgam of messianic eschatology and garbled historical events. He believed the Jesus of the Bible was loosely modeled on the life of the Teacher of Righteousness.

No doubt the Catholic members of the Scroll team were horrified when they began to decipher the texts. They could see how the Scrolls could cast doubt on the Biblical stories of Jesus, and their response was to keep the Scrolls away from the outside world, including other scholars. Allegro accused them of intentionally suppressing information in the texts that contradicted official Christian dogma. Indeed, the secrecy was maintained for more than 40 years, until photographic plates of the documents were secreted out of their possession and distributed to scholars around the world.

Before we try to untie the knot created by this conflict, we should examine other mentions of reincarnation that made their way into the official canons of the New Testament. For example, in Luke (1:11-17) there is the story of the Jewish priest, Zechariah, who was also visited by an angel and told that his aged and barren wife, Elizabeth (a kinswoman of the Virgin Mary), would "bear a son, and thou shalt call his name John...and he shall go before the Lord in the spirit and power of Elijah..." This John, the reincarnated Elijah, would grow up to become John the Baptist who would play an important role in the Jesus story.

Elijah, of course, was one of the ancient Hebrew's greatest Old Testament prophets, remembered as the one who was carried into heaven in God's chariot of fire (2 Kings 2:11), (think UFO) while walking with his successor, Elisha. It says: "And as they went on and talked, behold, a chariot of fire and horses of fire separated the two of them. And Elijah went up in a whirlwind into heaven."

Elijah was known for being an overzealous follower of Jehovah. During a confrontation with Canaanite priests over whether Jehovah was stronger than their god, Baal, Elijah had 450 of their prophets put to death by the sword. (1 Kings:18-17-40) He was beheaded by King Herod in his new life as John the Baptist, perhaps to balance the negative karma he created in that life,

In Matthew 11:9-16, we find these interesting words of Jesus as he speaks to his disciples about the Old Testament prophecy by the prophet, Malachi, referring to John the Baptist:

"Yea, I say unto you, he is more than a prophet. For this is he of whom it is written, 'Behold, I send my messenger before thee.' Verily, I say unto you, among them that are born of women, there hath not risen anyone greater than John the Baptist...and if ye will receive it, this is Elijah, who was to come.... He that hath ears to hear, let him hear."

Here we have a clear example of Jesus teaching his disciples about reincarnation. Additionally, Jesus matter-of-factly infers that there are those who are born of women (humans) and those who are not—a reference to angelic beings who are above humans in the hierarchy of life in the universe. Among the Essenes, these super-human beings were known as the Watchers. Jesus always refers to himself as the son of man, and never claims to be God.

Other examples of Jesus teaching his disciples about reincarnation are found in the book of Matthew. In Matthew (16:13-14), Jesus asks his disciples, "Whom do men say that I am?" They answered, "Some say that thou art John the Baptist, some say Elijah, and others Jeremiah, or one of the prophets." Clearly, it was commonly believed that Jesus was the reincarnation of a great prophet, if this passage is accurate. But an interesting sidebar to this example is that the writer (supposedly Matthew) didn't know that John the Baptist was a contemporary of Jesus, meaning Jesus could not possibly have been John in a previous lifetime. How could Matthew not know this? Or, to say it another way, how could whoever wrote or edited the book of Matthew not know this? The passage is a major example of the inaccuracies found in the Bible of today.

We can see in these examples that not only was reincarnation a concept well known at the time of Jesus, but it was a topic of conversation among the First Century Jews. It leaves us wondering why, if the Bible so clearly states that reincarnation was accepted by Jesus and his followers, is it not included in the Christian doctrines of today, and why is it not discussed in Sunday sermons or in Bible study classes in both Catholic and Protestant Churches? And, they leave us wondering how these passages made it into the Bible in the first place? The answer is simple. The Councils that established the veracity of the ancient texts weren't concerned that people would actually read the Bible because almost everyone was illiterate. Later, the Church had the Bible translated from ancient Greek into Latin, again because very few people could read Latin, thus giving the Church control over the "Word of God." Possession of an "unlicensed" Bible (one translated into a vernacular language) carried a death sentence, and, in fact, in 1536 William Tyndale, an English Bible scholar and linguist, was strangled and burned at the stake for translating the Bible into English.

Today's Catholic and Protestant authorities simply choose to ignore the passages referring to reincarnation, or they use convoluted reasoning to explain them away. Additionally, for centuries everyday Christians have simply not studied the Bible critically, but rather have read it for inspiration, accepting wholeheartedly what they have been told by Church leaders. Christians have for so long accepted by blind faith the notion that the Bible is the written word of God, that they do not bother to question that assertion.

There is one other reason that the general public does not understand these problems with the Bible—the true history of Christianity and the Bible texts is so complex that it takes years of careful study to truly see the whole truth—a truth most would probably rather not know.

Now, back to the dilemma posed by the similarities between the Essenes and the early Christians, and between Jesus and the Essene Teacher of Righteousness. This is a serious, more than 2,000-year-old mystery that cannot be easily resolved by Bible scholars, and certainly not by a journalist such as myself, so I can only express my best guess as to the truth of the matter.

Part of the answer was given me during a 1995 past-life regression I underwent during the time I was taking a certification course in hypnotherapy. Quite unexpectedly, as the hypnosis progressed, I suddenly had a vision of a wooden crucifix, floating like a 3-D image right in front of my closed eyes. Then, the cross leaned away from me and took off like a jet plane, pulling me along behind it. Suddenly, the cross was gone and my consciousness was hovering over a beach, and on the beach were a number of clay jars lined up neatly on a very dry shore. Tiny waves, full of froth, were gently lapping on the beach, and I knew this was the Dead Sea and that those very distinctly shaped jars contained the sacred scrolls of the Essenes. I remember being puzzled. Why was I being shown this? And what did the crucifix have to do with the Dead Sea Scrolls? I had no idea. And then, the therapist conducting the hypnosis asked me two leading questions in rapid succession. "Was this at the time of Jesus? Did you know him?"

Those questions essentially ended the session as I burst into tears. It was as if a tsunami of terrible emotions slammed into me, and I sobbed like I had never sobbed before. After a few minutes, I opened my eyes and came out of the trance. I just couldn't go on; I just couldn't bear to re-experience the emotions of grief, sorrow, anger and guilt that the tsunami hit me with. It was too much to bear. Over the years I tried to recover memories of that past life with different therapists, without feeling those emotions again, but all I received was the idea that I was somehow responsible for keeping my "brother" safe, but failing. It was as if I was begging him not to go into Jerusalem for Passover because it was too dangerous. But he couldn't be swayed. It was as if he knew he would be killed. It was like suicide by crucifixion.

The regression did, however, answer a question about my childhood that had always been a mystery to me and my family. As a child, beginning about the age of four and continuing to about the age of nine, I had an irrational fear of a crucifix that was affixed as signage to a church on a major thoroughfare in our city of El Paso, TX. Anytime we passed it at night, I would be overwhelmed with horrible feelings of sadness. At night, the outline of the cross was lit with blue neon lighting. Whenever I saw it, I would begin to scream and cry; to avoid looking at it, I would fall to the back-seat floorboard and curl up in the fetal position. At first, my parents thought it was so strange, they would laugh. But soon, they began to realize it was a serious matter. Rather than taking me to a psychologist, they agreed to tell me in advance when we would be getting close to that church so I could hide on the floor in the back seat, thus avoiding the problem. It was a compromise; previously I had begged my dad not to pass by the church by using another street to get wherever we were going. My dad found that idea too cumbersome, as it would require making a time-wasting detour. No one ever thought the problem could be caused by a past-life trauma. No one in our mostly Catholic community believed in reincarnation, but my case is one example of how a past-life trauma can affect a person in a present life. Such traumas can manifest themselves in many ways—as phobias, illnesses, pain and even beliefs.

In summary, my personal experiences and my research have led me to conclude that Jesus was an Essene, as was his "kinsman," John the Baptist. They were both raised by the Essenes as children and taught to read the sacred scrolls so they would be ready to go out into the world and proselytize when they became adults. Jewish historian Josephus wrote that the Essenes were known for taking in boys to teach them their ways. German scholar Otto Betz wrote that John the Baptist was probably raised at Qumran and must have lived there during his early years and later left to preach directly to a wider community of Jews. (Shanks 1992, p. 206).

Let's return to the puzzling knot created by the Dead Sea Scrolls, the Essene Teacher of Righteousness and the Biblical Jesus. My conclusions are based not only on my personal experiences, but also upon the many years of research I have undertaken to discover the truth about the connection between the Scrolls and the life and death of Jesus.

Firstly, I am convinced that John Allegro is correct about the Essene belief that their messiah was the reincarnation of the Prophet, Joshua/Jesus, even though he believed the Teacher of Righteousness lived much earlier than the time of Christ, a conclusion with which I disagree. Discovering that Jesus's name originates in the Essene belief that their messiah would be the reincarnated Joshua, solves a two-millennia-old mystery about where the name "Jesus" came from, but that also means that Jesus was the Teacher of Righteousness written about in the Scrolls. What better appellation could there be for the Jesus of the Bible? That means that the Scrolls tell the true story of Jesus and

At night, the blue neon around the cross frightened and saddened me terribly when I was a child. It was a sign of a past-life trauma.

(Author's photos)

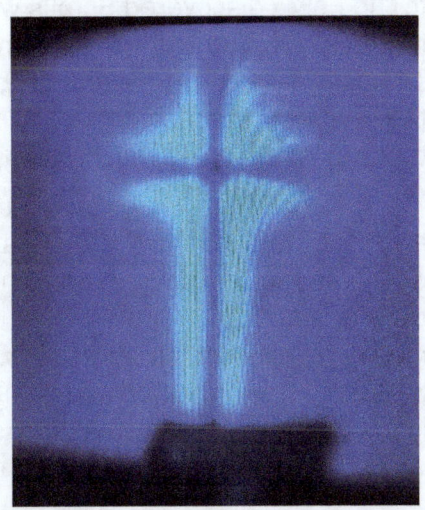

that the New Testament books are greatly exaggerated, and contain mythical tales, written long after Jesus died on the cross. It also means that Jesus did not die to save us from our sins, as Christians today are told, but rather he came to save us from being trapped in the vicious cycle of reincarnation by teaching us how to live our lives in an enlightened way. The implication is that planet Earth is a place of punishment and imprisonment (Hell if you wish to call it that) for souls who have not learned their lessons of unconditional love, and charity toward their fellow humans.

Secondly, we have to ask why the Catholic priests, who controlled the Scrolls for so many years, refused to let anyone else see and study them. Clearly, they knew all too well that the ancient documents would cast serious doubts on the stories of Jesus in the New Testament. Everything they had been taught and believed about the Bible was seriously challenged, and they understood the damning implications the Scrolls held for all of Christianity, and particularly for the Catholic Church. This brings up a very basic question that not even Bible scholars have dared ask: Could Catholic priests be considered unbiased scholars in this instance? Could they possibly examine the documents in a scholarly and unbiased, scientific way? Clearly, the answer is a resounding *no!* The worst thing that could have happened to the newly discovered Scrolls would be to put them in the hands of the Catholic Church, which quite possibly secreted some of the most damaging ones away to be locked up in the deepest recesses of the Vatican archives. We're lucky that any of them ever saw the light of day.

Thirdly, we now know, thanks to diligent Bible scholars, that the books of the Bible are not accurate accounts of events that happened more than 2,000 years ago. The truth is that the Scriptures were tampered with and bear many inconsistencies and errors. They cannot be the genuine, inerrant words that God wanted to convey to us. The fact is that there are no original books of the New Testament, which Bible scholars have known for many years. Graduates of theological seminaries are acutely aware of this problem, but most go on to become clerics, choosing to ignore or somehow overlook this most serious issue, and preserve their faith.

Again for confirmation, read *Misquoting Jesus* by Dr. Bart Ehrman. Ehrman holds a Ph.D. from the Princeton Theological Seminary, and is someone who has spent a lifetime learning to read the ancient Greek, Latin and Aramaic languages. He has translated the earliest-known texts to learn the truth for himself. He serves as the James A. Gray Distinguished Professor of Religious Studies at the University of North Carolina, Chapel Hill, and is a leading authority on the Bible and the life of Jesus. He is the author of more than 20 books, some of which have been on the New York Times bestselling list.

Ehrman, who started his Bible studies truly believing the Bible was the word of God, gradually became disillusioned as he realized that the New Testament books cannot be relied upon to be factual. After studying the most ancient texts in Aramaic, ancient Greek and Latin, he saw that there was little agreement among them and that none of them was original. He finally concluded that much of the Scriptures were actually forged and were not really written by the authors named in the Bible. "I did my best to hold on to my faith that the Bible was the inspired word of God with no mistakes, and that lasted for about two years.... I realized that at the time we had over 5,000 manuscripts of the New Testament and no two of them are exactly alike. The Scribes were changing them, sometimes in big ways, but lots of times in little ways. And it finally occurred to me that if I really thought that God had inspired this text...why didn't He go to the trouble of preserving the text?"

These discoveries altered his religious beliefs, causing him to go from being an evangelical, faith-based Christian to an agnostic atheist. It seems that faith is a fragile thing, and we must be careful about what we hold worthy of our faith. If the words in the Bible cannot be the accurate words of God, then what can we believe in? Blind faith in forged documents, it seems, will not be enough to save us from the vicious wheel of eternal reincarnation, but perhaps there are some truths to hold on to. Because we cannot rely on the Bible to know the true story of Jesus, and because the Dead Sea Scrolls use titles for the Essene leaders, rather than proper names, we will never know the true story of the historical Jesus. However, there is a pattern that clearly emerges from these ancient texts. There was a belief in reincarnation and the concept of karma. Spiritual masters throughout history have all taught the same lessons about the law of cause and effect. So we can be fairly certain that some words from the Bible are truthful regarding the teachings of Jesus. Here are some:

"As ye sow, so shall ye reap."

"Judge not lest ye be judged."

"Love thy neighbor as thyself."

"He who killeth by the sword must be killed by the sword."

"He who leadeth into captivity, must also be led into captivity"

"Forgive those who trespass against you."

"Love your enemies."

These words give us a road map to real salvation, and they have nothing to do with religious dogma or blind faith.

Finally, the Scrolls contain what may be the most significant connection to the story of Jesus ever found. In The Thanksgiving Psalms, which contain 25 separate poems offering thanks to the Lord, who gave the community the secrets of salvation, are words some scholars believe to be written by the Teacher himself—Jesus. The psalmist is obviously a man of great spiritual knowledge (gnosis) and a leader of the Essene community. Some of these poems concern the torment the writer feels knowing he is hunted by his enemies, who would torture and kill him if he were found:

"I thank you O Lord, for your eye is awake and watches over my soul. You rescue me from the jealousy of liars, from the congregation of those who seek the smooth way (the Pharisees). But you save the soul of the poor whom they planned to destroy by spilling the blood of your servant."

"I walked because of you—they didn't know this. They laughed at me. They shamed me with lies in their mouth. But you helped the soul of the poor and the weak, you saved me from their harsh arms, you redeemed me amid their taunts. From the wicked I do not fear destruction."

"Teachers of lies have comforted your people and now they stumble, foolishly. They abhor themselves and do not esteem me through whom your wonders and powers are manifest.... They preach lies. They are dissembling prophets. They devise baseness against me, exchanging your teaching, written in my heart, for smooth words. They deny knowledge to the thirsty and force them to drink vinegar."

"You have had me live with many fishermen, spreaders of nets on the face of the water, and hunters of the children of error. There you established me for justice, and in my heart you fortified a counsel of truth and waters of the covenant for its seekers."

In Psalm 14, the Teacher seems to foresee his own demise:

"My wound breaks out like fire in my bones, day after day, turning me feeble, chewing my flesh. Gone is my body strength, my flesh melts like wax, the power of my loins is terror, my arm is torn from its socket, worthless, my knees slide in the water, my feet are shackled, unable to walk, my tongue—which you made marvelous—is tied! I cannot talk, I cannot lift my voice to my disciples to encourage with words those who are stumbling. My circumcised lips are still."

8

The Watchers

Among the Dead Sea Scrolls are books of the Old Testament, (many of these are kept at a museum in Israel), books about the Essene community that lived at Qumran (the people who studied, copied and kept secret the sacred scrolls), books which are commentaries on the books of the Old Testament, and some that tell the stories of life on Earth before a great flood destroyed much of the civilized world. Most of these latter scrolls found their way to the French Bible School, a Catholic institution, which appointed a small group of priests to study and translate the texts.

Among these last books were some translated by Fr. Josef Milik, a Catholic priest, one the original team members. These are known as The Books of Enoch. Interestingly, there are more copies of the Books of Enoch among the scrolls than any other category except those of the Old Testament. Thus, the Essenes must have held them in very high regard and considered them as sacred as the Biblical texts.

Enoch, it is said in Genesis 5:21-24, was one of the descendants of Adam, and the great-grandfather of Noah. Enoch is said to have lived in the antediluvian days when angelic beings were on the Earth intermingling with humans. These beings are known as the Watchers—those who watch over Planet Earth and its inhabitants:

"Now a population explosion took place upon the Earth. It was at this time that the beings from the spirit world looked upon the beautiful Earth women and took any they desired to be their wives.... In those days, and even afterwards when the evil beings from the spirit world were sexually involved with women, their children became giants (known as Nephilim) of whom so many legends are told." (Genesis 6:1-7).

The mention of Enoch and the Watchers in Genesis reveals that whoever wrote the Old Testament books also held the Books of Enoch sacred. But the Bible doesn't tell the whole story of the Watchers, who were believed to be guardians of life on Earth. Enoch describes the Watchers as the "Angels of the Lord" who "come down to Earth to instruct the children of men and to bring about justice and equity on earth." But in the case of the evil angels, the science they teach turns to wicked ends because of their sin, which is that they permit their sexual appetites to dominate them. "When the sons of God saw the daughters of man, they could not restrain their inclination." (Milik, 1976, p. 327).

One of Enoch's books is titled "The Book of the Watchers," which describes a conflict between two opposing forces of seemingly even powers: the good Watchers and the evil Watchers. The evil Watchers are those who broke away from the good Watchers and mated with human women. The evil Watchers abused their power as custodians of the physical world by taking liberties with their human chattel and bearing children with them, much as today's aliens are believed to be creating hybrid species by mixing human DNA with their own, sometimes through sexual intercourse.

Finally, the evil Watchers fall from grace with God when Enoch is taken up to heaven to testify against them. He tells God that the Watchers "had begun to go unto the daughters of men, so that they became impure." As punishment for their sins, God destroys humanity, including the hybrid race of beings (the Nephilim), by causing a great flood, and punishes the evil Watchers by putting them in a fiery pit.

They are imprisoned by the four chiefs of the good Watchers, the archangels Michael, Sariel, Rafael, and Gabriel.

No doubt the Essenes had a strong belief in the existence of the Watchers, angelic beings who warred against each other in the heavens, and who could come down to Earth in physical form. They saw this epic battle as the war between beings of light and beings of darkness, and they decidedly took the side of those of the light. In fact, they refer to themselves in the Scrolls as the "Sons of Light,"—the representatives on Earth of the good Watchers. Their enemies were the representatives of darkness on Earth—the Roman rulers and their puppets, who controlled the Jerusalem Temple—the Pharisees.

Instead of naming the high priest of the Temple by name, the Essenes, for security's sake, referred to him only as the "Wicked Priest," whereas in the Bible he is called out by name: Caiaphas—the one who had Jesus arrested and turned over to the Roman authorities. Also called out by name was Pontius Pilate, the Roman official who presided over the trial of Jesus. Why did the New Testament writers feel free to use proper names, while the Essenes did not? It had to be because they were writing long after these officials and their successors were dead—long dead.

The New Testament writers had to have been writing about history, many years after the actual events took place. We know that in the years after the crucifixion, Jerusalem was in great turmoil. Resentment toward the Roman and Jewish authorities had been brewing for many years, and it finally erupted in violence and mayhem in the form of a Jewish revolt around the year 66, only 36 years after the crucifixion. The revolt was brutally put down by the Romans in the years 68-70, during which Jerusalem and the Temple were completely destroyed and tens of thousands of Jews were massacred, including the Essenes and their community on the shores of the Dead Sea. During those 36 years after the crucifixion, Jesus's followers were scattered or killed. It was hardly a period conducive to sitting down and writing the stories that we find in the Bible today. As for the Essenes, evidence indicates that they hastily buried their sacred scrolls in the caves around Qumran, expecting to come back for them later, but that day never came. The Essenes were among the many thousands of Jews who were killed, their history forgotten for nearly 2,000 years.

The Qumran scroll jars

9

Jesus: Man or God?

As early Christianity evolved, there were many Christian sects, each having its own favorite books and beliefs about the life and ministry of Jesus. In the aftermath of the horrible torture and death of their spiritual leader, we can only imagine the confusion and turmoil that descended upon his disciples. In fear for their own lives, they hardly had time to sit down and write about their experiences and their beliefs about the life of Jesus. Most of them, being of humble origins, could not even read or write. Besides, Jesus had told them he would be back soon—within their own lifetimes.

Historian Josephus described the scene in 68-70 AD by saying that the Romans left Jerusalem a pile of rubble. So it is not surprising that the first written stories about the life of Jesus did not appear until several decades after the crucifixion, when it became apparent that he was not coming back anytime soon. Bible scholars theorize that the first writings were simply lists of quotations or sayings based on what people remembered about what Jesus said or preached. These texts were lost to history, but they are referred to by scholars as the book of "Q".

The theory states that the authors of the texts we now know as the New Testament used this mysterious lost book of "Q" as the basis for their own writings, but by then most of the true story of Jesus was lost to history. His followers in the decades after his death tried to reconcile the reality of what happened to him—being put to death like a common criminal—with the idealized notions they still had about what they thought was supposed to have happened. After all, he had told them that the Kingdom of God was coming soon, and all wrongs would be righted. Instead, he was arrested, tortured, and murdered. The overly zealous came up with aggrandized stories—myths—to explain away the horrible end to their beloved teacher. There had to be some mysterious meaning underlying this disaster that would explain why it all ended so badly. The notion that Jesus really didn't die——he resurrected from the grave!—emerged from the need to find meaning in the otherwise unexplainable turn of events, And furthermore, even if he did die, his death had meaning—great meaning. His sacrifice on the cross was given a spiritual purpose—he died to save us from our sins!

Books about Jesus abounded in the early decades after the crucifixion, written by unknown hands, and few in agreement with the others. Some purported to tell stories of the nativity, while others, more fanciful, told about his childhood and are known as the Infancy Gospels. But there were huge gaps in the story. Nothing was written, or is known, about where he was and what he was doing between the ages of about 12 and 30. Wouldn't God want us to know all the facts? One would think so. There are very few reliable facts in those texts, and there are no original copies of any of them. Bible scholars and historians understand that what we know now as "orthodoxy" emerged gradually over the 300 years after the crucifixion. It took that long for any kind of consensus to be reached among the disparate views that existed among those who sought to turn the story of Jesus into a new religion—a religion that Jesus, himself, never wanted. He was a Jewish rabbi, albeit one whose teachings did not align with those of the Pharisees, who controlled the Jerusalem Temple of his day.

Nevertheless, there were those who were determined to create a new religion, and thus ensued a long and turbulent battle for control over the story and meaning of his ministry. Each sect sought to be recognized as the true Christianity, with much of the disagreement centered on the issue of the divinity of Jesus: was he just a holy man, a great spiritual teacher, or was He God incarnate? The story of Jesus and his life became confused and in disarray by the time his surviving followers began to piece together what it all meant. There were those who believed that Jesus was a great teacher—a holy man, and there were those who believed he was a divine being, perhaps the son of God. Then there were the extremists who wanted to declare Jesus God Incarnate. How would these disparate views ever be reconciled? Or perhaps there was no need for reconciliation. Why not just let people believe what they wanted to believe? Well, that idea just did not sit well with the Roman authorities who, above all, required an orderly society.

It took the boot heel of Roman Emperor Constantine (285-337 AD) to finally decide the issue. After failing to wipe out the Christian faith through persecutions that included feeding Christians to the lions for the entertainment of its citizens, Roman authorities finally agreed to the acceptance of Christianity as a religion. It seemed that Christianity wasn't going away; in fact, the Roman people began to admire and sympathize with the brave Christians who would rather die than give up their faith. The movement was growing, but it wasn't exactly clear what Christianity was. There were so many conflicting views, so many conflicting texts, and so much dissension among the different sects that, finally, in June of 325, in an effort to obtain some measure of consensus, pagan Emperor Constantine gathered together over 300 bishops, representing the various sects, to a meeting in the Greek town of Nicaea, to hash out their differences. This is known as the first Ecumenical Council of Nicaea.

The stimulus for such a meeting was the growing belief in the teachings of the ascetic Alexandrian priest, Arius, (250-336) who taught that Jesus had been a man, a holy prophet, but not "co-eternal" with God. Jesus, he said, was subordinate to and distinct from God. He believed Jesus

Constantine

was promulgating a new version of Judaism, not creating a new religion. These ideas found a large following throughout the Roman Empire, and created a large schism between themselves and those who wanted to see Jesus as God. His opponents argued that Arianism was polytheistic because it made Jesus equal to the mythical demigods worshiped by Rome. Additionally, Arius argued that those who had denied Christ to save their lives due to the threat of torture, should be readmitted to the Church—a position that was anathema to the orthodox view espoused by the opposition leader, Alexander of Alexandria.

    Of course, Arius and his followers lost that debate at Nicaea. He and two other bishops refused to sign the resulting document and Arius was banished from the empire. Later, he was arrested and tortured for his heretical views, dying from his wounds in 336—a stark example of what was at risk for speaking against the prevailing view. It was at Nicaea that a vote was held declaring Jesus God Incarnate. All other views and texts not agreeing with that belief were declared heretical. Thus was born the beginnings of the Orthodox Church and today's Roman Catholic Church. The role of the Emperor in the proceedings was not one of a spiritual nature, it was more like that of a referee, who was determined that a consensus be reached for the sake of keeping the peace. His presence at the Council was also to ensure that whatever was decided would be in the best interest of the State. Political control of the masses was his agenda, and the resulting vote of the Council participants, he hoped, would put an end to the constant bickering about what Christianity actually was. His concerns regarding the issue of reincarnation were based on a mistaken belief that if people believed they would be born again, they would not worry about breaking the laws in their present lives.

Although the issue of reincarnation was not debated at Nicaea, the fallout for all dissenting views was widespread. All texts that did not agree with the decision, including what we now know as the Lost Gospels, or the Gnostic Gospels, were declared heretical, forcing many bishops to flee for their lives. Among those many texts in circulation were those that portrayed Jesus as a man, rather than a god, those that espoused reincarnation, and those that said that all humans are divine. An important result of the Council was the requirement that all Christians must accept and recite what is now known as the Nicene Creed, which reads as follows.

"I believe in one God, the Father almighty, creator of heaven and Earth... I believe in one Lord, Jesus Christ, the only Son of God, born of the Father...begotten, not made... For us men and our salvation he came down from heaven, and by the Holy Spirit was incarnate of the Virgin Mary, and became man. For our sake he was crucified under Pontius Pilate, he suffered death and was buried, and rose again on the third day in accordance with the Scriptures. He ascended into heaven and is seated at the right hand of the Father.

He will come again in glory to judge the living and the dead, and His kingdom will have no end.
I believe in the Holy Spirit, the Lord, the giver of life, who proceeds from the Father and the Son.... I believe in one, holy Catholic and apostolic Church. I confess one baptism and the forgiveness of sins and I look forward to the resurrection of the dead and the life of the world to come."

Constantine then wrote a letter to all bishops who had not attended the Council, requiring them to accept the Divine Will of the majority. He then began a systematic persecution of dissident Christians by issuing an edict against heretics and forbidding them from assembling in any public or private place. Their houses of prayer were to be given to the Orthodox Church. Constantine ordered a search for their books, which were to be destroyed. Anyone hiding the works of Arius could be put to death.

But as frightening as this edict was, the debate over reincarnation was not over by any means, and Christianity had not yet been declared the official religion of the Roman Empire. Nevertheless, the Nicaean Council's declarations had widespread ramifications. The Creed required that all Christians accept that Jesus was God Incarnate, not just a holy man. It required Christians to accept that he was born of a virgin, that he was crucified for our salvation, that he rose bodily from the dead, that he will come again to judge the living and the dead, that he gave, through his apostles, the right to claim that there is only one true church—the Catholic Church, and that because of him, the dead will rise from their graves on the day of judgment.

Later, in Protestant churches, the creed was amended slightly and is called the Apostle's Creed. But even that creed declares Jesus as the only son of God, creating a deep demarcation between humans and Jesus (God). In both Churches, humans are separate from God, rather than being gods trapped in human bodies, who can achieve "godhood" through a process of seeking spiritual knowledge and becoming enlightened.

These Creeds are a lot to ask of people to accept on blind faith, yet many millions recite this Creed every time they attend a Catholic mass or Protestant service. Their adherents don't bother to ask, "Where do these ideas come from?" The answer from the Church is that all of these ideas come from the Scriptures. The Council members created the Creed based on those texts they believed were the most accurate, those inspired by God, those they liked the best, and those they could use to gain control over the new religion.

But, there is just one problem with this reasoning. We know that there are no original texts of the Canonical Bible. No one can possibly know the true story of Jesus. The error in the Church's claim that they relied on Scripture to formulate their Creed can be seen clearly by anyone who examines the first four books of the New Testament, which are ascribed to the apostles Matthew, Mark, Luke, and John, but in actuality were written by unknown hands. Each of these books describe what happened on the most important day in Christian history—the resurrection of Jesus from his tomb.

If we read these books carefully and with a critical eye, we find some remarkable inconsistencies. Matthew writes that early on Sunday morning, Mary Magdalene "and the other Mary" went out to the tomb. Suddenly there was a great earthquake; for an angel of the Lord came down from heaven and rolled aside the stone and sat on it. Then the angel told them that Jesus wasn't there and bid them to enter the tomb to see for themselves where his body had been lying. Then he told them to go quickly to tell his disciples that he has risen from the dead, and he is going to Galilee to meet them there. As they ran from the tomb, suddenly Jesus appeared to them and told them, "Go tell my brothers to leave at once for Galilee to meet me there."

Mark's Gospel tells a similar tale, but in his narrative there are three women who go to the tomb: Mary Magdalene, Salome and Mary, the mother of James. He makes no mention of an earthquake and he reports that the tomb was already open when they arrived. When they enter the tomb, they see a young man clothed in white, who tells them that Jesus is alive and on his way to Galilee. Mark's book says that Mary Magdalene was the first to see the resurrected Jesus, but he doesn't describe the encounter.

The Gospel of Luke, on the other hand, says that the three women who went to the tomb were Mary Magdalene, Joanna and Mary, the mother of James. In his version the tomb was already open when they arrived, but the tomb was completely empty. Luke's version has Peter and two other followers of Jesus being the first to see Jesus, and it is not Galilee, but Jerusalem where they go to find the disciples.

Finally, the Gospel of John gives yet another account of the events. "Early Sunday morning, while it was still dark, Mary Magdalene came to the tomb and found that the stone was rolled aside.... She ran and found Simon Peter and me and said, 'They have taken the Lord's body out of the tomb, and I don't know where they have put him!'" Peter and John then run to the tomb and John gets there first. When Peter arrives, they enter the empty tomb and examine Jesus's linen burial cloth. Then they go home. Then Mary returns to the tomb and finds two white-robed angels on the place where Jesus had been lying. Finally, "She glanced over her shoulder and saw someone standing behind her. It was Jesus, but she didn't recognize him. When she finally recognized him, she reached for him, but Jesus warned her: 'Don't touch me, for I haven't yet ascended to the Father. But go and find my brothers and tell them that I ascend to my Father and your Father, my God, and your God.'"

It is obvious that all of these versions describing the singular most important event of the New Testament present great problems for those who preach that the Bible is the unerring word of God. They each tell a different version of events, and they can't all be right. Who was the first to reach the tomb? Was it Mary Magdalene alone, or was it Mary Magdalene and the "other Mary?" as Matthew says.

Or was it Mary Magdalene, Salome, and Mary, mother of James, as Mark says? Or could it have been Mary Magdalene, Joanna, and the mother of James, as Luke reports? John says Mary Magdalene alone went to the tomb. Was the tomb open or closed? Were there angels present? Who is the first to see the resurrected Jesus, Mary Magdalene or Peter and two other men? Where was Jesus going to meet with the disciples? Was it Galilee or Jerusalem? Was there an earthquake as reported by Matthew, but not by the other witnesses? Why didn't Mary recognize Jesus when she first saw him, and why wasn't she allowed to touch him? Was he in physical form, or was he an apparition?

There was not one person at the Council of Nicaea who could reasonably answer these questions, yet they supposedly used Scripture as their basis for declaring that Jesus was God. It is easy to see why Dead Sea Scroll scholar John Allegro, wrote in *The Dead Sea Scrolls and the Christian Myth*:

"The Gospel stories that have come down to us in the New Testament canon are, of course, only a small part of the mythical literature circulating in the various messianic sects, which proliferated...in AD 68. It is clear that the so-called Great Church, early on, purged the stories of elements it considered unsuitable, or which would hinder the movement's acceptance by the authorities, Jewish and Roman, who threatened its survival."

Regardless of the conclusion of the Council, many Christians continued, and still continue, to believe in reincarnation as the foundation of the teachings of Jesus. Even Church father St. Augustine, Bishop of Hippo (353 - 430) conceded in his book, *The City of God*, that it is better to be ignorant of reincarnation than to know the truth:

"What pious souls could bear to hear that after a life spent in so many and severe distresses...that this will happen endlessly, again and again, recurring at fixed intervals, and in regularly returning periods? ...Who, I say, can listen to such things? Were they true, it were not only more prudent to keep silence regarding them, but even to express myself as best I can, it were the part of wisdom not to know them... why should we now increase our misery, already burdensome enough, by the knowledge of them? ...now, at least let us remain in ignorance...since in this life we are expecting to obtain life everlasting, but in the world to come are to discover it to be blessed, but not everlasting."

Yes, St. Augustine accepted that reincarnation might be true, and that life on Earth is like a living hell, but he felt it is better to be ignorant of it, for our peace of mind. It was this kind of obtuse thinking that ruled among those seated in the Councils of Constantine, causing books that revealed sacred knowledge to be deleted from the official Canons of the New Testament. However, it took more than 200 years after the Council of Nicaea to end the debate about reincarnation in the new Orthodox Church. In the year 553 at yet another council—the Second Council of Constantinople—the idea of reincarnation was declared to have no place in the doctrine of the Catholic Church. Here it was decided that the early Church Fathers who taught reincarnation would have their writings banned, declared heretical, and, thus, destroyed. Among those books were those of Valentinus, Basilides, Origen of Alexandria, and others who had been influenced by the writings and teachings of Greek philosopher Plato.

Once the Councils had concluded their work, Christianity was legitimized by the Roman state, and once again, all books not condoned by the Roman Emperor were declared as false. Anyone having them in their possession was declared a heretic and could be put to death. Thus, much of what, in the earliest days of Christianity, was thought to be sacred, was lost to history. That is until nearly 2,000 years later, in 1945, when workers near the town of Nag Hammadi in Upper Egypt accidentally uncovered a cache of ancient texts, known today as the Lost Gospels, or the Gnostic Gospels.

10

The Gnostics

The Gnostic Gospels, apparently written by disciples of Jesus, were among the many books declared heretical by the Council of Nicaea and the later Councils of Constantinople. "Gnostic" is derived from the Greek word "gnosis", meaning knowledge—sacred knowledge, the kind one can only receive in visions or in altered states of consciousness.

Because the texts were discovered buried close to an ancient Christian monastery near the Egyptian town of Nag Hammadi, it is believed that they once belonged to monks who, fearing for their lives should they be caught with them, buried them in a red, earthenware jar, under a large boulder. The jar contained 13 papyrus books, bound in leather. Within the books were 52 texts, some bearing the names of Jesus's disciples: *The Gospel According to Thomas*, *The Gospel of Philip*, *The Secret Book of John*, *The Secret Book of James*, and *The Gospel of Mary Magdalene*—none of which are to be found in today's Bible. Some scholars believe that the writings may be older than the Gospels of the New Testament, and equally as valid. No doubt they are also copies of copies, rather than originals. Critics complain that we don't know who really wrote the documents, but that criticism rings hollow when we understand that the same can be said of the canonical texts.

The Gnostic view of spirituality is summarized succinctly in *The Gospel of Thomas* with these words:

"If you bring forth what is within you, what you bring forth will save you. If you do not bring forth what is within you, what you do not bring forth will destroy you."

These words could be used by a modern-day hypnotherapist who employs past-life regression techniques to help his client resolve debilitating issues in his present life, as I previously mentioned.

The Gnostics also used meditative practices, not dissimilar to hypnosis to discover what was within them and to make a direct connection to the divine. There was no need for an institution or priests who believed they were the intermediaries between humans and God. The Gnostics, in effect, went over the heads of the priests and bishops to find God for themselves.

The Lost Gospels/ Nag Hammadi texts

One of the longest of the Gnostic texts, *Zostrianos*, describes the procedure for attaining enlightenment. First, one had to remove physical desires for the purpose of practicing an ascetic life. The initiate cleansed his mind and spirit to eliminate the "chaos in the mind." This he did under the guidance of a spiritual master. In this quiet, meditative state, the initiate could receive visions and revelations from the divine. These revelations most certainly would have included past-life memories.

Other Gnostic documents propose that there are levels of insight the initiate must reach before achieving gnosis. They recommended using chants made of sacred words or vowels, similar to the tones used in what we could call transcendental meditation today. One of the objectives of reaching the highest altered states was to achieve an out-of-body experience. In a text called *Allogenes*, the author reports that while out of body he saw "holy powers" that gave him knowledge. "I knew myself as I am.... I received power.... I knew the One who exists in me."

Elaine Pagels, Princeton professor of religion wrote in *The Gnostic Gospels* that "such a program of discipline, like the higher levels of Buddhist teaching, would appeal only to the few.... The methods of Gnosticism did not lend themselves to mass religion. In this respect, it was no match for the highly effective system of organization of the Catholic Church...which offered a creed requiring the initiate to confess only the simplest essentials of faith...." In other words, Catholicism won out over Gnosticism because it was so easy for anyone to become a Catholic and so difficult to become a Gnostic. (Pp. 140-141.)

What further separated the Gnostics from the orthodox view was their belief that Jesus did not come to save us from our sins (they did not believe in original sin), but rather to serve as a guide to spiritual knowledge.

It is easy to see why Gnostic teachings were deemed heretical, for they describe Jesus more as a man than God—

one who was in love with and kissed Mary Magdalene on the mouth, much to the consternation of the other disciples, particularly Peter, who held Mary in particular disdain. In the Gospel of Mary Magdalene, it is Mary who takes the leadership role after the crucifixion, rather than Peter. Terrified and depressed, the disciples ask her to tell them what Jesus taught her secretly, and she agrees. But Peter objects to the teachings, asking angrily, "Did he really speak privately with a woman and not openly to us?"

Levi comes to Mary's defense, saying, "if the Savior made her worthy, who are you...to reject her? Surely the Lord knew her very well, that is why he loved her more than us." In yet another text, *The Pistis Sophia*, Peter again complains that Mary is dominating the conversation with Jesus, and he asks Him to stop her from speaking, but Jesus refuses. Mary tells Jesus that she is intimidated by Peter because, "He hates the female race." Jesus sides with Mary and assures her that whoever is inspired by the Spirit, whether man or woman, is divinely ordained to speak. Such a view is antithetical to the orthodox doctrine, which only allows men to serve as priests.

Another book found at Nag Hammadi, *The Dialogue of the Savior,* portrays Mary as one of the three disciples who received special teachings from Jesus. Of the three, which included Thomas and Matthew, Mary was said to have been the prize student: "...she spoke as a woman who knew the All." Mary says, in her own Gospel that Jesus appeared to her in visions and ecstatic trances after his death. Yet, when she ran to tell the other disciples what had happened, she says that "Andrew and Peter did not believe her." She describes the tension between her and some of the other apostles. In this case, Peter was suspicious, not only of the testimony of a woman, but also of the notion that one could see the Lord in visions. Peter is portrayed as being literal minded, while Mary and a few other disciples are shown to be more spiritually minded.

In the Gnostic texts we find a completely different version of the story of Jesus—one that does not conform to the orthodox, male-dominated Church we know today. Had the Gnostics prevailed, women would have a much more prominent role, even the ability to lead congregations. Peter would not have been considered the successor to the teachings of Jesus, and the foundation of the Orthodox Church may have crumbled. The idea that Jesus bodily resurrected may not be part of the Church's dogma, but rather that the disciples saw the deceased Christ in visions, dreams or altered states. This process is the foundation of the Gnostic belief system—much of which was not lost entirely, even though the texts were declared heretical.

The notion that Mary was the true inheritor of the teachings of Jesus was carried forth secretly into the Middle Ages and the Renaissance. For example, in Leonardo da Vinci's celebrated painting of the Last Supper, found in Milan, Italy's Dominican monastery, Santa Maria della Grazie, Peter is shown hiding a dagger behind his back and threatening a female figure seated next to Jesus, believed to be Mary Magdalene, with his other hand. The idea that Jesus and Mary were actually married, as heretical as that may be to the Orthodox Church, is still alive today among those who lean toward the teachings of the Gnostics.

The Gnostics believed, as did the Essenes, in angelic beings, variously called Watchers, Sons of God, Aeons, or Archons, and that it was the Archons who forced souls to reincarnate by putting them in "fetters" and sending them back to Earth to be born of a woman. One of the Nag Hammadi texts deals directly with the Archons. It is titled *The Hypostasis of the Archons* (The Reality of the Archons), which could also be interpreted as "The Reality of the Rulers", or "The Nature of the Rulers". In any case, the document's purpose is to describe the reality of the Authorities of the powers of darkness, who are in opposition with the forces of light. The chief Archon is referred to variously as Samael, Sacla (fool) or Ialdaboth, who proclaims himself God, but is blind and mistaken. These Rulers of the material world were said to have created humans in hopes of entrapping souls: "The Rulers laid plans and said, 'Come let us create a man that will be soil from the Earth." They called the man Adam, and then they created a female from Adam's rib, as in the Book of Genesis. Then the Rulers put them in a garden that they might cultivate it and watch over it. "And the Rulers issued a command saying: From every tree in the Garden shall you eat, yet from the tree of Knowledge of Good and Evil, do not eat, nor touch it, for the day you eat from it, ...you are going to die."

But after they disobeyed and ate the fruit, a spirit in the form of a serpent came to them and said, "With death you shall not die, for it was out of jealousy that they said this to you. Rather, your eyes shall open and you shall come to be like gods, recognizing evil and good." The serpent in this version of Genesis, then, is the representative of the powers of light, who is helping the human race understand the trap they are in, pointing out to them that they are, in fact, gods. But when the Archons hear of this, they put a curse on the serpent: "From that day, the snake came to be under the curse of the Authorities... Moreover, they threw Mankind into great distraction and into a life of toil, so they might be occupied by worldly affairs, and might not have the opportunity of being devoted to the Holy Spirit."

The Hypostasis of the Archons tells a story similar to that found in the Bible, but with a startling twist. The serpent in this version is the hero, while the creators of Mankind are the villainous Archons—a concept at the core of the Gnostic belief system.

The Lost Gospels provide us with an insight into a lost form of Christianity—a form that set it firmly apart from the Orthodox view. The Gnostics, although Christians, did not believe that Jesus came to save us from our sins, but rather he came to serve as a guide to spiritual knowledge. Those who attain enlightenment through knowledge would become like Jesus—free of the bonds of the physical world. They believed that Jesus wanted us all to become like him, and that once we did, we would become his equals. He didn't come to save us from our sins, but rather, from our ignorance. He revealed to them that humans suffer from amnesia when he told them, "You are like the blind. You don't know where you came from, you don't know why you are here, you don't know what you are to do while you are here, you don't know where you will go when you die, and you don't know what will happen when you get there." But how are people supposed to know the answers to these provoking questions? There is only one way—by going within oneself and connecting to the divine by means of a meditative, altered state of consciousness. The Gnostics believed that enlightenment could only be achieved when a person discovered the answers to these questions. This is what is meant by the term "know thyself."

We have already seen examples of my hypnotherapy subjects who discovered why they were claustrophobic, or why they harbored ill will for the Catholic Church and Jesus, or why they feared dying alone, or why they were being abducted by aliens, or who they were in past lives, thus finding the answers to those provocative questions Jesus posed to his disciples. These people, desperate for answers that would resolve their problems, submitted themselves to hypnotherapy, and in the process discovered their direct connection to the divine, just as the Gnostics did two millennia ago. One can only imagine what the Jewish authorities thought of this aspect of the secret teachings of Jesus. He was teaching people that they didn't need the priests to find God. These teachings would have been seen as heretical and worthy of a death sentence. The foundations of Judeo-Christian teachings of today maintain that God and man are separated by a great void, and that only a few chosen ones (priests) have the ability to receive His revelations.

In contrast, Jesus tells his disciples, "Anything I can do, you can do also." By teaching his disciples the mysteries of spiritual healing and the secrets of the soul, Jesus was constantly urging his followers to follow his path, which is known as "The Way." In John 10:34 he told them, "Ye are gods! Thus prodding them to recognize their own divinity. This idea that humans are generally unaware of their own divinity is a frequent theme in the Lost Gospels of the Gnostics.

Their understanding of the cosmos was quite different from that of their orthodox contemporaries. The orthodox view is that God created the material world, but the Gnostic belief was that it wasn't God, but an inferior being known as the Archon or Demiurge, who in his ignorance believes himself to be God. This flawed being is unaware of his true origins, and thus he fashioned the material world in his own flawed image. The Archon is served by an army of beings, variously called Archons, Watchers, Authorities, or Sons of God. It is their task to rule over the physical world and to prevent its inhabitants from learning about their true, divine nature, thus imprisoning them on Earth in a cycle of reincarnation. If humans understood they were divine, they would know that as gods, their destiny is to reunite with the true God.

In the *Secret Book of John*, the apostle John describes a vision he had of the resurrected Jesus in which Jesus explains the cycle of life and entrapment of the human soul. John asks Jesus, "Christ, the souls...when they come out of the flesh, whither will they go?"

Jesus answers, "To a place for the soul. The righteous soul escapes from the works of wickedness and...will be saved and raised up to the rest of the Aeons." (Angelic beings).

John then asks, "Those who have not known the All, whither will they go?" Jesus answers, *"Those souls are delivered to the powers, which are under the Archons. The souls will once more be cast into fetters and led about until they are saved from lack of perception, to attain knowledge, and so will be perfected and saved.... (Then they) no longer go into another flesh."*

It is little wonder that the Orthodox Church banned and declared heretical the texts found in the Lost Gospels, for they clearly describe the role of the Archons in the process of reincarnation. For the writers of these books, Planet

Earth was clearly considered to be Hell. Being born as a human was to be put in chains over and over again repeatedly until the soul gained spiritual enlightenment. But enlightenment isn't easy, for the Archons plan includes placing many obstacles in a soul's efforts to "know the All." The first obstacle involved erasing their memories of past lives. Then, they created a place where souls would be assaulted by all manner of distractions, preventing them from spending too much time seeking spiritual growth. This notion is clearly presented in Genesis (11:1-9) when the creator gods saw the people building the tower of Babel:

"Look, the people are united, and they have one language.... Now nothing will stop them doing what they take in their minds to do. Come on let us go down there and confuse their language so they cannot understand one another's speech."

Here are some of other distractions keeping us from seeking spiritual truth: the ego (self-importance), sex, wars, different races, different religions, different nationalities, genocide, money, greed, different genders, terrorism, fashions, status seeking, natural disasters, television, iPhones, iPads, computers, social media, relationships, false teachings, blind faith, and authoritarianism, to name a few. The Archons have done a good job. With all that we humans must contend with, it's a wonder that we have any time left to seek true spiritual growth. We have so little time to devote ourselves to tending our souls, that most people just delegate that vital task to others—clerics, priests, preachers, Bible study groups led by people who don't understand the Bible, and televangelists. Delegating spiritual growth to others is exactly what the Archons want us to do. They delight in the fact that so many of us just take it for granted that our holy books are the inerrant word of God. That is a serious mistake, for we now know that is not the case.

Amazingly, there is one Gnostic sect that survived the pogroms, and it is still in existence primarily in southern Iran, Syria and Jordan. They are known as the Mandaeans, whose holy book *Creation of the World and the Alien Man*. The basic theme of the document is the idea that the human race is an alien race, estranged from its true home, which exists in another dimension. Their belief is that we humans are exiled here from our true home—the realm of light. The material world, they believe, is the world of darkness. The Mandaeans believe that the physical universe is a place that entraps beings of light (us) into physical bodies, and that to be human is to live in exile and to endure the anguish and terror of being separated from the King of Light (God).

Salvation comes through sacred knowledge that teaches that these dispersed particles of light must be gathered and restored to the original unity. The Mandaeans believe the Archons are serpent beings—angels of darkness whose mission is to create chaos on Earth, and to maintain the illusion that the physical world is real, so that humans will believe in the falsehood of materiality and separateness. (Barnstone, pp. 123-141)

Indian-American author and alternative medicine advocate, Dr. Deepak Chopra, once said something that caught my attention: "God gave us spirituality, and Satan packaged it and sold it to us as religion."

Is it possible that the Archons are behind the great religions of the world? That is exactly what many Christians in the Middle-Ages believed, that is, until they were massacred by the Catholic Church's strong arm—the Inquisition.

11

The War on Reincarnation

It wasn't until 553, during the Second Council of Constantinople, that the doctrine of reincarnation was finally found to have no place in Christian teachings. The idea was not officially rejected, but those early Christian leaders who espoused reincarnation had their works banned, thus ending the official debate within the Christian community.

One might ask: "Why is reincarnation such a threat to the orthodox view?" There are two answers to this question: first, it threatens the idea of the bodily resurrection of not only Jesus, but of all humans on the Day of Judgment, when Jesus is to return. Obviously, reincarnation did not require the bodies of the dead to spring back to life. Resurrection, to Gnostics, refers to the release of the spirit from its human body, only to be reincarnated into a new body, born of a woman. Secondly, reincarnation threatens the orthodox view that Jesus's death on the cross was a sacrifice that God made for the purpose of redeeming our sins. Those who taught reincarnation believed that Jesus did not come to save us from our sins, but rather to save us from the vicious cycle of reincarnation, and thus, to save us from our ignorance.

One might also think that the Roman Emperor's declarations threatening adherents of the concept of reincarnation with torture and death would have been enough to finally do away with such heretical views, but that was not the case. Those edicts were only the beginning of the war against reincarnation and other heretical views. The Councils may have put an end to public discussion of the issue, but it never really went away—it just went underground. There were many who privately decried the violent means by which the Church and State tried to stomp out opposing views, and resentment toward the Church and its corrupt leaders and priests caused widespread grumblings throughout the Empire. Anti-Catholic groups met covertly as the Western Roman Empire crumbled, and the seat of its power moved from Italy to Constantinople (now Istanbul), a city in what is now Turkey, founded by Emperor Constantine in the year 330.

The Western Roman Empire finally collapsed in 476, ushering in what we know today as the Dark Ages—900 years of ignorance, illiteracy and strife. Historian William Manchester, in *A World Lit Only by Fire*, describes those centuries as "...a mélange of incessant warfare, corruption, lawlessness, obsession with strange myths, and an almost impenetrable mindlessness... Intellectual life had vanished.... Even Charlemagne, the first Holy Roman emperor, was illiterate." It was a turbulent time, one apparently ripe for the expansion of Catholicism, but not without much turmoil and confusion. In 1054, during what is known as "The Great Schism," The Catholic Church split in two as a result of theological disputes. Thus was born the Eastern Orthodox Church, based in Constantinople, with the Roman Church remaining based in Rome. This rift continues to the present day, each one still hurling epithets at the other on occasion, and each claiming to be the true inheritors of the teachings of Jesus. It is little wonder that the people who lived in these confusing times were open to new teachings, and a different form of Christianity, based on purity, equality of women, and spiritual knowledge.

There were those from all over Europe, or Christendom, as it was then known, who had not abandoned the teachings of the Essenes and the Gnostics. It is believed that some of their texts survived in hidden places, and their beliefs continued to be taught secretly. By the Seventh Century, a Christian sect known as Paulicianism flourished in Armenia. Their adherents referred to themselves as "Good Christians," as opposed to Catholic Christians, whom they referred to as "Romanists." The "Paulicians" were thought to be the followers of the teachings of Paul, the Apostle, who never knew Jesus, but became a follower of Christ through a vision. This, by definition, made Paul a Gnostic—someone who received "gnosis" by means of a divine revelation. This connection to the Apostle, however, is speculation. Some historians believe that there could have been another leader named Paul who has been lost to history.

Some scholars believe Paulicians were influenced by earlier sects, such as Marcionism, Manichaeism and Adoptionism, but this is also more speculation than fact. Nevertheless, it is known that the sect flourished between 650 and 872 on the outskirts of the Byzantine Empire in Armenia and Eastern Anatolia. But, as happens to moths when they fly too close to the flame, Paulician leaders were arrested and tried for heresy by the Catholic authorities, and either stoned to death or burned at the stake around 690. More persecutions caused them to flee further into Armenia, while others were forcibly relocated to the Balkan frontier in Thrace. Finally, after prolonged battles with the Byzantine Catholic authorities, the sect was all but wiped out in the 870s.

However, that was not the end of challenges to Catholic dominance of Christian beliefs and the teachings of Jesus. There was no greater example of the rise of "heresy" during the early Middle Ages than what occurred in the southwest of what is now France, along the coast of the Mediterranean. Amazingly, some 500 years after the Second Council of Constantinople, in the middle of the Dark Ages, there grew Christian movements that taught reincarnation, and stood defiantly as an alternative to Catholicism. Its adherents were known as the Albigensians, a name derived from the name of the city of Albi in what is now southwest France, but at the time was not part of France, but rather an independent territory known as the Languedoc, meaning "the language of Oc." The word "Oc" was short for "Occitan," a long-lost language spoken in that area at the time.

From the mid-1100s until about 1244, the Albigensians, or the Cathari, (meaning the purified ones), as they preferred to be called, practiced a form of Christianity that began to rival the Catholic Church in popularity. To deal with

The Cathars were forced to wear this emblem by the Catholic authorities, just as the Nazis required Jews to wear the cross of David.

the threat, the Church first tried to reason with and convert those whom they thought had gone astray, but when that didn't work, the Church resorted to violence. In the year 1209, Pope Innocent III launched the Albigensian Crusade to wipe out their heretical beliefs. Naming himself Innocent did not make him innocent.

But who were the Cathars and what exactly did they believe? Because there was no institution unifying the movement, few records exist, other than those of the Inquisition and the Catholic persecutors at the time. In Andrew Phillip Smith's *The Lost Teachings of the Cathars*, Smith quotes from a 13th-Century Catholic author who describes one of the key heretical views of the Cathars: "the heretics postulated two creators, to wit, one of the invisible world, whom they called the benign God, and one of the visible world, or the malign God. They ascribed the New Testament to the benign God, the Old Testament to the malign one; the latter book they wholly rejected..." (p.3)

This idea, known as dualism (a distinctly Gnostic belief), would explain why bad things happen to good people; it points out the obvious differences between the wrathful and tyrannical God of the Old Testament and the loving, merciful God of the New Testament. The Cathars, as well as many people today, could not understand how a good God could allow so many bad things, such as natural disasters, murders, genocides, torture and executions to happen to the innocent, particularly children. They reasoned that there had to be another power in the universe intent on causing havoc on Earth. They believed it was this evil God and his minions who created the physical universe and the human race. This belief was, of course, antithetical to the monotheism preached by the Catholics, as stated in the Nicene Creed: "There is one God, creator of all things, visible and invisible."

The Cathars, who referred to themselves as Bons Hommes (Good Men) or Bonnes Femmes (Good Women), identified the God of the Old Testament as Satan, while the

Catholics embraced the Old Testament and made it part of their Bible.

Additionally, the Cathars believed in reincarnation—that human souls were angels trapped in the material world of the evil God. Souls were destined to be reincarnated until they achieved salvation by living ascetic lives and by receiving a blessing they called the "Consolamentum," a ritual akin to a Catholic priest administering baptism or Holy Communion, but performed by the Cathar leaders, known as the Perfecti. Tobias Churton, writing about the beliefs of the Cathars in *The Gnostics*, quotes the second century theologian, Clement of Alexandria, who wrote about the meaning of gnosis: "The knowledge of who we were, and what we have become, where we were, or into what we have been thrown, whither we hasten, from what we are redeemed." (P. 74)

Churton concludes, "This was precisely what the Cathar Perfecti did teach. They taught that the souls of angelic beings had been stolen by Satan and put into the bodies of men...." The ritual of Consolamentum then was for the purpose of helping an initiate to release his soul from the grip of the Devil's material bondage, and re-uniting it with the Holy Spirit, thus becoming a Perfecti as well.

The Perfecti were men and women who had achieved enlightenment and perfection by having lived lives of asceticism, eschewing sex and other temptations, as well as being strict vegetarians. They were men and women who had known "The All," meaning they knew about their past lives and the reality of the Archons. The ritual consisted of prayers, the laying on of hands, and placing a copy of the Gospel of John on the heads of "believers," as well as those close to death. (It is possible that the Cathars had in their possession copies of the banned Lost Gospels, particularly the Secret Book of John, which describes John's vision of the resurrected Jesus, in which Jesus reveals to him the cycle of reincarnation and the powers of the Archons.) At the end of the ritual, the initiate, known as a "believer," would be instructed to reject the Roman Catholic Church, its promises and its sacraments; then he or she would become a Perfect, the highest level of Catharism.

It is reasonable to posit that the Cathar Perfectsi also practiced the Gnostic methods of attaining spiritual enlightenment. How else would they achieve their goal of perfection and knowing The All?

Cathars also believed that the Catholic rituals of baptism and Holy Communion had no spiritual value. They decried the act of Communion, which requires its followers to believe that they are actually receiving the body and blood of Christ, in the form of a wafer and a sip of wine, as an

Pope Innocent III

empty ritual, with no spiritual value, in comparison to their ritual of Consolamentum.

Finally, the Cathars believed, much as the Gnostics did, that Jesus was a holy man, divine, but not God incarnate. Many even believed that Jesus and Mary Magdalene were married, a commonly held view in the Languedoc region at the time.

Clearly, this increasingly popular competitor to orthodoxy—one with such radically different beliefs—could not be ignored or abided by the Catholic Church. It was a movement that the Roman Catholic Church feared more than any other as its most dangerous competitor. The Church, which had, in the year 1095, organized the first Crusade against Islamists in the Holy Land, found it only natural to turn its armies, not against Islamists, but against Christians who dared to teach a form of Christianity diametrically opposed to orthodox beliefs.

In 1209 Pope Innocent III sent an army of Crusaders to attack the heretics in a series of battles, which, in fact, turned out to be massacres. On July 22 of that year, the feast day of Mary Magdalene, who was revered in Southern France, the crusaders invaded Beziers, whose population of about 10,000 included only 222 Cathars. The Catholic bishop of the town refused to turn over the Cathars to the army, so the order was given to enter the city and kill the heretics. Because there was no way for the soldiers to distinguish Cathars from its Catholic inhabitants, the leader of the army, Arnold Amaury, was reputed to have said: "Kill them all. God will know his own." Within three hours the siege was over with more than 15,000 men, women and children slaughtered. More than 1,000 citizens who huddled in the church of Mary Magdalene seeking safety, were butchered by knives and bludgeoned by clubs, including Catholic priests who were saying mass. Then, the town was torched and burned to the ground.

In the ensuing years, the armies of Pope Innocent III wiped out the towns and cities of the Languedoc, massacring and pillaging without care about who it was they were killing. In 1210, after raiding the town of Carcassonne, they attacked the town of Bram. After the battle, they took 100 Cathars on a 20-mile forced march to the town of Cabaret. But before setting out, they cut off all their noses and upper lips and blinded them, leaving one, who was not blinded, to lead the way. That same year 140 Perfecti were burned at the stake in the town of Minerve.

The following year 80 defenders of the town of Lavaur were hanged and 400 Cathars were burned at the stake in a huge conflagration. In the town of Les Casses, 50-100 Cathars were burned and in 1219, more than 7,000 inhabitants of the town of Marmande were slaughtered by an army led by Prince Louis of France. In 1229, an inquisitorial body was created specifically to deal with the problem of the Cathars, first in the Rhineland, (another Cathar stronghold), then in the Languedoc.

In 1244, French armies stormed the mountaintop stronghold of Montesegur and burned 225 Perfecti. The final battle occurred in 1255 at Queribus, where after a three-week siege, the city fell and the French soldiers stormed through the gates to rape, murder and pillage.

The atrocities caused an unknown writer to pen "The Song of the Cathar Wars" about one of the leaders of the Pope's armies, Count Simon de Montfort, which said in part: "If by killing men and shedding blood, by damning souls and causing deaths, trusting evil counsels, by setting fires, destroying men...by seizing lands and encouraging pride, by kindling evil and quenching good, by killing women and children, a man can in this world win Jesus Christ, certainly Count Simon wears a crown, and shines in heaven above."

Count Simon de Monfort
(Wikigallery.org)

12

The Inquisition

In 1184, the Roman Catholic Church instituted the first of a series of inquisitional bodies charged with suppressing heresy in response to movements within Europe considered to be a danger to Western Catholicism, particularly the Cathars and Waldensians in southern France as just discussed. Today, the Inquisition resides in a Catholic body called The Sacred Congregation for the Doctrine of Faith, a vital part of the Church's everyday affairs. It oversees the curricula of Catholic schools, investigates heresy, judges threats to the faith, disciplines priests, excommunicates sinners, and even appoints exorcists.

A heretic was—and still is—defined as anyone who believes, teaches, or feels that he could have or has had a direct relationship with God, without the authority of the Church. If such persons do not renounce that belief and return to Catholicism, they could, even today, face excommunication, but in the Middle Ages, most likely they would face life imprisonment, torture or death by hanging or burning at the stake.

This inquisition remained active for a century, spreading terror throughout the region. The battles over, and the Cathars defeated, France then annexed the Languedoc, making it a French territory. The inquisitors, who could be likened to the Church's secret police, would wreak havoc in Europe for centuries more. The first Inquisitor mandated by Pope Gregory IX to deal with the Cathars was Conrad of Marburg, who was responsible for the deaths of hundreds of thousands of heretics and Catholic peasants who were caught up in the violence. Then, to the horror and great dismay of the people of the Languedoc, the Inquisitors arrived in 1233, with the goal of smothering any stray "embers" of Catharism that still yet remained hidden amongst the population. The inquisitors, friars of the Dominican Order, ensconced themselves in the towns of Toulouse, Albi and Carcassonne, endowed with the powers of arrest, trial, torture and execution of any heretics who would not recant their faith and return to Catholicism.

Perhaps the most famous and notorious of these Inquisitors was Bernardo Gui, who wrote a comprehensive manual for Inquisitors, and who established his base at a

Bernardo Gui

Dominican convent in Toulouse in 1306, which became known locally as "Le Hotel de Inquisition." Gui was made famous, or rather notorious, in author Umberto Eco's *The Name of the Rose,* and later a movie of the same name in which Gui was portrayed frighteningly by academy-award winner, F. Murray Abraham.

Andrew Phillip Smith, in *The Lost Teachings of the Cathars*, describes the techniques used by the Inquisitors to identify and punish heretics:

"Inquisitors traveled in pairs, (the tip of) a clandestine bureaucracy that was similar to the Soviet KGB or East German Stasi. Scribes and clerks recorded and filed the confessions. Legal apparatchiks, constables, bailiffs, attorneys, prison wardens, torturers and executioners enacted the institutional violence on which the Inquisition's theological-dogmatic edifice was founded.... It was persecution on an industrial scale.... When Inquisitors arrived in a town... the entire population was summoned to a public assembly. Anyone who held a heterodox belief was expected to confess there and then, and absence from the assembly was seen as an immediate admission of heretical guilt.... Those accused of being Cathars, or suspected of having connections or sympathies, were questioned carefully...."

Sometimes, each and every villager would undergo a terrifying interrogation, being pressured to name Cathar sympathizers on pain of death. They were expected to tell on their friends, neighbors and even family members. Pointing fingers at others could lead to a death sentence being commuted, or could be the difference between a long prison sentence and merely being forced to wear a yellow cross sewn on their clothing, just as Jews were forced to wear the Star of David on their shirts by the Nazis. The yellow cross was a sign of a social pariah—a stigma affecting the person's social standing. The Inquisitors searched every possible hiding place in every building, including cellars, attics, and outbuildings. Perfecti who were found were burnt; sympathizers were forbidden from holding any kind of public office and were required to attend a Catholic Mass and go to confession every Sunday for the rest of their lives.

Thousands of Cathars were executed in the 13th and 14th Centuries, but many who escaped went underground, disguising themselves by living un-Catharlike lives or by hiding in huts deep in the forests. But the persecutions only strengthened Cathar beliefs among the population: that the material world was created by Satan and that the Roman Church was his Church.

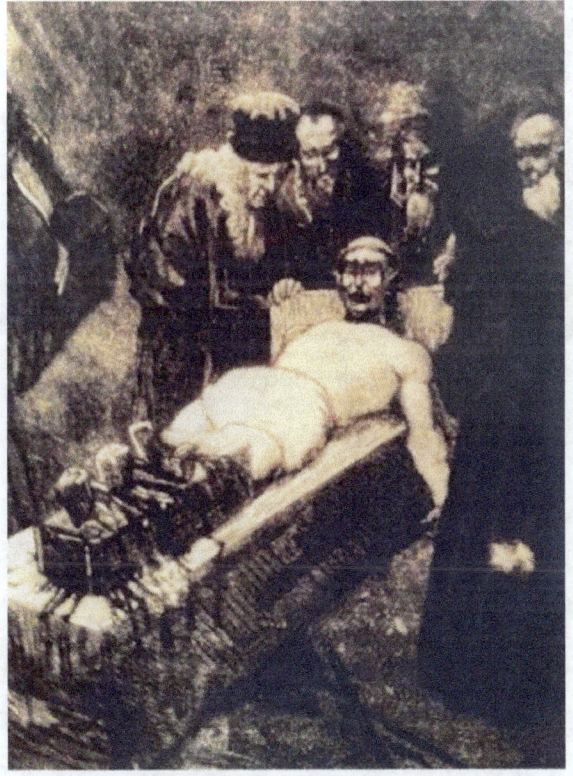

An Inquisition torture chamber

Cathars burned at the stake

13

Regulating Karma

The first Tibetan Dalai Lama was Gedun Drupa, who lived from 1391-1474. At his death, a council of high lamas began a search for his reincarnated soul in the form of a young boy. Word was sent out for lamas to be on the lookout for precocious boys who could possibly be the reincarnated Gedun Drupa. The search involved looking for signs, such as the direction the wind blew the smoke of his cremated body, showing them the direction in which they should look. Even dreams of high-council members were considered. Candidates, all young boys, were examined and tested by the committee of lamas, and some were taken to the temple where the Dalai Lama had lived. There, they were taken to a room containing various objects, some of which belonged to him and others of which did not. The children who were drawn to the articles belonging to him were primary candidates for the post of the new Dalai Lama. The council then, through prayer and meditation would make the final decision. This process, used each time a Dalai Lama died, often took years to conclude.

In 1793, an additional element was introduced into the process. In cases where there was more than one candidate, lots would be drawn from a special Golden Urn. The purpose of this was to include another element of fate into the process, and to prevent any cheating or corruption by members of the council or powerful families, wishing to have their child placed in the powerful position as political leader of their country.

Because the traditional political structure of Tibet is theocracy, with the Dalai Lama as its head, this most-important lama is both the religious and secular leader of the country. Thus the process of reincarnation and designating a new Dalai Lama is as much about choosing a new head of state as it is a religious leader—a non-democratically elected one. This fact created a dilemma for the Chinese government after its invasion of Tibet in October 1950, which China declared was an effort to liberate the Tibetan people by instituting a more effective way of choosing a leader—one aligned with communist/atheistic principles, of course.

Tibetans were against any interference by China in their process of selecting a new Dalai Lama and a new Panchen Lama, Tibet's other spiritual leader, known as the "great scholar," who is second in command and whose reincarnation follows the same process as the Dalai Lama. Each one serves on the council that seeks to find a replacement for the other, when the other dies. Today, the 89-year- old 14th Dalai Lama, Tenzin Gyatso, lives in exile in India, but is still held to be Tibet's leader by Buddhists around the world.

The 14th Reincarnation of the Dalai Lama

Even though he signed an agreement with the Chinese government in 1951, he later repudiated it on the grounds that he had signed it under duress. In 1959, during an uprising against the Chinese occupation, he fled to exile in India. His second in command, the 11th Panchen Lama, was recognized by the 14th Dalai Lama on May 14, 1995. Three days later, the six-year-old boy was kidnapped by the Chinese government and his entire family was taken into custody. He has not been seen in public since 1995. To replace him, China named Gyaincain Norbu as the 11th Panchen Lama, a nomination widely rejected by Buddhists in Tibet and abroad.

In 2007, China's State of Administration of Religious Affairs announced Order No. 5, a law covering "the management measures for the reincarnation of living Buddhas in Tibetan Buddhism," a move to institutionalize management of reincarnation, which prohibits Buddhist monks from returning from the dead without government permission, and allowing only monasteries inside China to apply for permission. So now, the Chinese totalitarian state is trying to control not only the lives of their subjects, but also their souls. This law seems laughable because regulating the destiny and karma of a person's soul through government regulations is patently impossible. However, the Chinese really don't care about souls, as they don't believe such things exist; they just want to control the political leaders of Tibet by being the ones who choose the next Dalai Lama. It appears the Chinese government is not opposed to religion, *per se*, but only to religions it cannot control.

What has been the reaction of the current Dalai Lama to the Chinese reincarnation laws? His public statements on the issue have been purposefully vague or misleading. At first, he said there is a chance that he might choose not to reincarnate, but if he should, it would not be in a country under Chinese rule. This is because Article 7 of the Chinese laws on reincarnation states that "no group or individual may carry out activities related to searching for and identifying the reincarnated soul of the living Buddha without authorization."

Subsequently, making it even more difficult for the Chinese to find a reincarnated Dalai Lama, he said the next time he could possibly be a woman. In 2011, he issued a statement concerning his reincarnation, giving the exact signs on how the next one should by chosen, including the place of rebirth, and that any Chinese-appointed Dalai Lama should not be trusted.

Regardless of what happens after the death of the current Dalai Lama, it is apparent that there is a mind-boggling contradiction regarding the atheistic Chinese government's attempts to control the afterlife and reincarnation of Tibetan monks. By doing so, they are openly admitting that the soul exists and that it can be reborn, even though the Communist Party is officially atheistic and officials are barred from practicing religion.

Another important issue never mentioned is the matter of the soul's ability to choose its future path. Certainly the Tibetans believe it does, but as we have seen, there are powerful entities in the afterworld who are ultimately in charge and who will decide where, when and under what conditions a soul will reincarnate. As we will see in the following chapter, these beings, called "The Masters," by Dr. Brian Weiss's hypnotherapy patients, play a central role in deciding what should become of a person's soul in the future.

14

The Masters

Thus far we have seen that the beings we call "aliens" or "extraterrestrials" today have been called by many names in the past: demons, angels, archons, aeons, watchers, visitors, rulers, and even the Sons of God, in the Bible. In every case they are known to have amazing powers, allowing them to intervene in human affairs at will, and with great stealth. In many cases, they are seen as the creators of the material world and life on Earth. In far-away lands, such as Australia, the aborigines painted cave walls 10,000 years ago with renderings of beings that look amazingly like the Gray aliens of today. These beings, referred to as the Wandjina, are revered as creators of the material world. Among many North American Indians, they are known as the Star People, and are believed to be their ancestors. In some European cultures, they are elves, the little people, the wee ones, fairies, incubi, or succubi.

What they are called depends on the culture and the perspective through which people see the world. In ancient times the lens through which people observed the world around them was religion, while today, it is technology. Many American researchers today tend to see the phenomenon through the lens of science and the scientific method, and they conclude that the beings are people from other planets. They are so tied to the materialist world view that they

Aboriginal rock art depicting Wandjina
From the Barnett River, Mount Elizabeth Station, Australia
Photo: Graeme Churchard, Bristol, Courtesy Wikimedia Common

deduce that the beings are evil, with an agenda to take over the world. In other cultures they are seen as angelic beings who are here to help the human race. Most likely their agenda is unknowable to humans.

But one man, who discovered beings who exist in another dimension, and who assist human souls to plan their next lives on Earth, calls them the Masters. Dr. Brian Weiss, author of *Many Lives, Many Masters* and other books about past-life regression hypnotherapy, was a mainstream psychiatrist, (much like Dr. John Mack). He had reached the highest levels of respectability and credibility within his profession. He graduated *Magna Cum Laude* from Columbia University, and subsequently, graduated from Yale University School of Medicine. Ten years later, he was serving as Chief of Psychiatry at Mt. Sinai Hospital in Miami and had published 37 scientific papers in medical journals. His commitment to mainstream science and to traditional psychiatric methods and theories ran deep, as did his concern for his reputation. As he states in the introduction to his book, "Years of disciplined study had trained my mind to think as a scientist and physician, molding me along the narrow paths of conservatism in my profession. I distrusted anything that could not be proved by traditional scientific methods."

But then one day, he began to treat a woman who had come to him for help in curing a number of disorders. He tried conventional psychotherapy for 18 months with no success. In desperation, he decided to try hypnosis, thinking that she might recall childhood memories that could be the cause of her problems. However, under hypnosis, the woman spontaneously recalled past-life memories which proved to be the cause of her symptoms. As she remembered past-life traumas, her symptoms improved dramatically. But that wasn't all. While in trance, she began to act as a conduit or "channel" of communication with spirit beings she called "the Masters," who were with her while her soul was in between lives. These Masters proceeded to reveal to Weiss many of the secrets of life and death. "Nothing in my background could have prepared me for this. I was absolutely amazed when these events unfolded," he said. Weiss was left with a shattered paradigm, but at first he was unsure how the experience would affect his practice.

Ultimately, due to the incredible healings he observed with his patient, and the lessons he learned from the Masters, he began using past-life regressions in his practice, with amazing results, but not without much trepidation. He worried that mainstream psychiatry would not approve of his methodology and that his credibility would suffer. He was right. Weiss had been transformed. As a result of his communication with The Masters, he was forced to reevaluate everything he had been taught about the nature of science, reality and religion.

Then, he decided to share his story, not only with his colleagues, but with the world. In 1988, Weiss published his first book on the subject, *Many Lives, Many Masters*, which detailed the work he did with his patient, and the lessons he had learned from the Masters. His decision proved costly. Upon the publication of his book, Mount Sinai Hospital failed to renew his contract, proving once again that the mainstream scientific community punishes those who stray outside the carefully defined consensus views of reality.

Weiss laid out the bizarre communications he had with the Masters while his patient was in a deep trance. The beings turned his world upside down when they informed him that the purpose of his patient's visits to him was for his spiritual enlightenment. "Suddenly she spoke, but not with the slow whisper she had always used previously. Her voice was now husky and loud, without hesitation." The Masters began explaining the rules of spiritual evolution:

"Our task is to learn, to become Godlike through knowledge.... By knowledge we approach God, and then we can rest. Then we come back to help others." Then, the Masters revealed to him information about himself and confidential information about his family, so as to prove to him their superior, transcendental knowledge. Gradually, the lessons became more advanced as they explained:

"There are seven planes in all...each one consisting of many levels.... On one, you are allowed to see your life that has just passed.... We have debts that must be paid.... You progress by paying your debts.... With each life that you go through and you did not fulfill these debts, the next one will be harder.... You choose what life you will have."

Weiss was stunned by such revelations, coming from a Christian woman who had no belief in Eastern philosophy or in reincarnation. He became convinced that the information he was receiving was from a higher spiritual level, rather than from her subconscious mind:

"I was acquiring a systematic body of spiritual knowledge. This knowledge spoke of love and hope, faith and charity. It examined virtues and vices, debts owed to others and to one's self. It included past lifetimes and spiritual planes between lives. And it talked of the soul's progress through harmony and balance, love and wisdom, progress toward a mystical and ecstatic connection with God. There was much practical advice along the way: the value of patience and of waiting; the wisdom in the balance of nature; the eradication of fears, especially the fear of death; the need for learning about trust and forgiveness; the importance of learning not to judge others...and perhaps most of all, the unshakable knowledge that we are immortal. *We are beyond life and death, beyond space and beyond time. We are the gods, and they are us."*

Astonishingly, the teachings of the Masters align perfectly with the beliefs of the Cathars, the Essenes, the Buddhists, and the Gnostics, but not with those of the orthodox Christian churches, or with mainstream Judaism. These sects/religions differ from the Western religions, which teach that people's sins condemn them to hell for all eternity, and that we have but one chance to make it to heaven. The lessons Weiss received from the Masters explain how life on Earth is actually fair—we have many opportunities to learn and grow, eventually working our way out of the material world. This new view of reality helped Weiss to walk away from his traditional therapy, and the hospital he worked for, to begin a new career as a best-selling author who lectures before large audiences conducting mass hypnosis sessions, helping people to remember their own past lives, and thus resolving problems and losing their fear of death.

Scientists have deduced that the material world represents only about 5% of the known universe. The rest is invisible, called dark matter and dark energy.

We know virtually nothing of what might exist in this other dimension. (Courtesy NASA)

15

The Andreasson Affair

Betty Andreasson Luca has had a life-long relationship with non-human entities she calls "The Watchers," whom she perceives as angels. Her story was first revealed in a book authored by UFO researcher, Raymond Fowler, called *The Andreasson Affair*, published in 1979. Fowler, a highly respected and meticulous researcher, was director of investigations for the Mutual UFO Network (MUFON), and had worked for 25 years with GTE Government Systems as a senior planner on major weapons systems, such as the Minuteman and MX missiles. His investigation of the Andreasson case is one of the few longitudinal studies, documenting one case over many years. He published Betty's continuing story in four additional books: *The Andreasson Affair—Phase Two, The Watchers, The Watchers II,* and *The Andreasson Legacy.*

Betty was born in 1937 in Fitchburg, MA, to a devoutly Pentecostal Christian family in which she was the second youngest of five children. In his initial interview with Betty, Fowler realized that, due to her strong religious upbringing, she was interpreting her experiences within the context of her fundamentalist Christian beliefs. She was certain that the non-human entities who had entered her home and taken her to an awaiting saucer-shaped craft, were angelic beings, which she referred to as Watchers. Fowler, while not dissuading her of this interpretation, found that her experiences were very much in line with typical cases of "alien abduction."

Fowler found that Betty's experiences started as an infant when a beautiful, tall blonde being would take her from her crib at night to a craft where physical examinations and operations were performed. Betty, and her husband, Bob Luca, who also had abduction experiences, interacted with the typical small Grays, as well as the human-looking Tall Blondes, who identified themselves as the "Elders" and who are in charge of the Grays. In *The Watchers*, published in 1990, Fowler records a hypnosis session in which Betty asks the beings who they are:

"He says that...they are the caretakers of nature and natural forms—the Watchers. They love Humankind. They love the planet Earth—and they have been caring for it and man since man's beginning. They watch the spirit in all things.... Man is destroying much of nature.... He's saying that they have collected the seed of man—male and female—and that they have been collecting...every species and every gender of plant for hundreds of years."

The Watchers explain to Betty that they exist in a timeless dimension where past, present and future are all one. They have demonstrated this by taking her on numerous journeys outside of her body into their dimension. She is made to understand that "man is not made of just flesh and blood." They further explain that their technology, one that combines science and spirit, permits them to co-exist with humans, to whom they are genetically related. Their long-term program of genetic manipulation is meant to prolong and improve life on this planet. This includes the use of surrogate mothers for the production of hybrid offspring. The program has been accelerated in recent years because the human race is to become sterile due to an environmental disaster on a global scale, which will lead to the death of life on this planet. They are taking steps to preserve Earth's life forms for existence elsewhere in the universe.

In his 1995 *The Watchers II*, Fowler reports on a hypnosis session in which Betty's husband Bob recalls a similar conversation with an alien entity who explained certain spiritual laws:

"You see, the body... is a shell.... The real you is the light person inside...the light force that does not die.... That's the real you.... That part advances through stages. Our existence here is only one of many steps in a long learning process.... We are all being monitored. Nothing you do in your life escapes them. It's just like a recorder.... All is recorded from the time you are born until the time when you die.... How you react, what you do...even your innermost thoughts, feelings and emotions.... This process determines how rapidly you will advance, what your next step will be, and what hardship you must undergo to deepen your understanding."

The therapist asks, "Are you saying that, at some level, life is fair?"

"Yes, life is wonderfully fair. Those of us in this plane just don't understand it. When you see a small child that becomes ill and dies, people weep.... They grieve for themselves. The child does not need to be here any longer. The child has already advanced, much as you would skip a grade in school.... People that are sick or injured...their faith is being tested. Their reactions recorded. This determines whether or not they need more teaching."

"What about evil?" Bob is asked.

"Without evil to overcome, the righteous could not advance and triumph," Bob replies. "It's all part of the system.... There must be suffering, because without these things, there would be no advancement."

"Are you saying that evil is positive?"

Bob responds, "Evil on the earthly plane is the negative aspect. Evil on the larger plane is part of the over-all plan that gives us all a chance to advance and rise above it.... Everything in nature...has a plus and a minus, a light and dark, a negative and positive, a good and a bad. It must be, for without some content of evil, there is no good. There can be no growth.... The Creator gave us a choice. We cannot use that choice unless we have two choices to make—evil or good."

The findings of Fowler in his extended research into the Andreasson case could be considered by some as the result of powerful imaginations, or simply delusions based on religious beliefs, except for the fact that the advanced wisdom communicated to Betty and Bob under hypnosis is consistent with the findings of other researchers, including myself, in many other cases.

What is truly amazing here is that it is possible to communicate with these higher beings telepathically while the subject is in a hypnotic trance. To put it clearly, the therapist is able to communicate with the beings through the subject while in a trance—something that I have done regularly, just as Dr. Brian Weiss has done with his clients. These conversations often reveal information about the universe we live in, which provides us a foundation for a new understanding of the nature of reality itself.

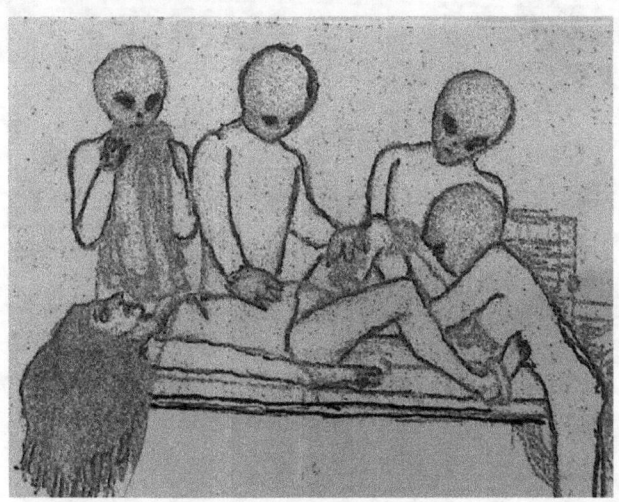

Delivering a hybrid baby

Illustrations from *The Watchers* by Raymond Fowler
(Bantam Books, New York, 1990)

Ascending into the craft

Illustrations from *The Watchers* by Raymond Fowler
(Bantam Books, New York, 1990)

Section III

Confirmation

16

The Tall Blondes

Early on in my investigation into the abduction mystery, I began to hear about the beautiful, tall, human-like beings, sometimes referred to as "The Nordics" or "The Tall Blondes." These beings were sometimes in the company of others, such as the Grays and the Mantises. Other types, or species, reported in abduction cases are those with reptilian features, and others difficult to classify. Determining the agenda of each type is difficult; there may be those who are trying to help humans, while others thrive on making life on Earth chaotic. I decided early on to simply dedicate myself to letting the facts speak for themselves, without casting judgment one way or the other.

The first cases I came across dealing with the Tall Blondes were in Mexico when I was invited to speak at a large, international UFO conference in Mexico City, in 1995. It was an exciting week; more than 30 speakers from around the world were assembled at a hotel near the huge auditorium at the medical school, where the conference was being held. Everywhere I turned, there were researchers and experiencers with amazing stories to tell. One of the speakers who caught my attention right away was a Mexican woman from the City of Puebla who videotaped dozens of strange aerial objects near her home, not far from the 18,000-foot active volcano, Popocatepetl, approximately 70 miles southeast of Mexico City. Her name was Dr. Soledad de la Peña.

Aside from the remarkable videos of UFOs taken in broad day light, her presentation intrigued me because she was exceptionally believable. She was a highly educated pediatrician who was recognized in Mexico as a reliable investigator and the leader of a team of researchers and experiencers who were armed with video cameras and constantly on the lookout for aerial phenomena seen frequently around the volcano. This was a case I found irresistible. I decided I had to go see what was happening for myself. After her presentation, I found her in the foyer of the auditorium and struck up a conversation in Spanish, which she appreciated, as she spoke little English.

Dr. de la Peña was in her mid-40s and obviously of Spanish descent, with very white skin and dark hair. She was very well spoken, and we hit it off without delay. During our initial conversation, she admitted to me that there was much more to her personal story than people knew. She had had many close encounters with non-human entities, including the Grays, since she was a child; she was clearly what we would call an abductee. But this case had a bit of a different twist. The reason, she explained, that she had so many videos of UFOs was because they let her know when they were in the area by causing her stomach to vibrate gently. She would then grab her video camera and dash up to her roof-top patio and begin filming. The objects were usually too high to make out details, but they were obviously not any type of recognizable aircraft. They would float gently in the air, going to and from the volcano.

I was so intrigued that I asked if I could visit her in Puebla sometime, and she readily invited me to come and stay with her and her husband, and to meet with her group. A few weeks later I made a special trip to spend a three-day weekend interviewing her and her team. They decided to take me to the base of the volcano where there was a vacant lot that served as a viewing area used by visitors to look for UFOs. A Japanese documentary crew had been there the week before, and other media from around the world had made the trip in the recent months. As soon as we arrived, the group set up folding chairs, and we made ourselves comfortable. Then I began to videotape interviews with them, one by one. It was a beautiful, cloudless afternoon, and the volcano, known locally as "El Popo," loomed very large in the background against the bright-blue sky. I discovered that it is one thing to see the snow-covered peak from a distance, but quite another to see it at its base. The closer we got, the more nervous I became. To make matters worse, for me, was the white, gigantic mushroom-shaped cloud rising thousands of feet into the air emanating from its peak. "Don't worry," I was told; "It's just steam; it's not ash. It's normal."

"Oh, is that all it is?" I responded skeptically. Somehow, that explanation didn't help relieve my anxiety all that much. As I tried to concentrate on the interviews, each of the seven group members told me about their sightings and experiences; they did not know about Dr. de la Peña's abductions, and I suspected that they were all being cautious about revealing their own personal stories. They were, however, eager to talk about other people's experiences from their own case files. Clearly, even in Mexico, there was a stigma associated with being an abductee, so their guarded remarks were understandable.

As the interviews progressed, I began to hear stories about the Tall Blonde beings who have interacted with people around the volcano. Even more interesting was the interpretation given of the UFO phenomenon and the alien beings that was expressed by the group. The prevailing theory was that the beings were not aliens, but celestial or angelic beings, and that they were not evil, but rather they were there to keep the volcano from erupting. (There are frequent news reports that "El Popo" has been erupting, spewing ash and rocks high into the air, and causing much consternation among those who live close by. A big eruption could consume not only the city of Puebla, but a good portion of Mexico City as well.)

They spoke about cases in which the beings were tall, with blonde, shoulder-length hair. They wore long white tunics with belts at the waist and sometimes with a box attached to the belt, which they took to be some sort of technological device. Then, in the middle of the discussions, a car pulled into the parking area, and a man got out and came over to our group. It turned out that he was the mayor of the nearby village and was well known to the members of our group, who greeted him cheerfully by name. After greeting him and introducing myself, I asked if I could conduct a video interview with him; he readily agreed.

"Have you seen any "OVNIs" yourself?" I asked. (In Mexico, UFOs are called "Objetos Voladores No Identificados," meaning, "flying objects not identified."

"Oh yes," he responded, without hesitation. "I have seen many."

"Have many of the villagers reported seeing them?"

"I would say at least 90% of them have seen them," he answered.

"What is the general opinion about what they are?"

"Most people say they are not aliens, but rather that they are from the celestial realm. They are angelic beings."

"Do you know anyone who has had contact with the beings?"

"Oh yes, I know several people who have told me about their experiences," he responded matter-of-factly.

"And what did they say?"

"They have described the tall, blonde beings with blue eyes. They are said to be quite beautiful and human-like."

"So the people in your village are not afraid of the OVNIs?" I asked.

"No, we are used to seeing them, and they mean us no harm."

I was surprised that the general view of the nature of UFOs and the beings who piloted them was so different from the way UFOs are regarded in America, where many researchers and experiencers regularly focus on the negative aspects of the phenomenon, particularly the covert aspect of their actions. Perhaps the way aliens have almost always been portrayed in Hollywood movies as being dangerous and evil could have something to do with that. Also, it was important to note that the people of Mexico are much more religious and tend to interpret unusual phenomena through the lens of their predominately Catholic upbringing. Unlike many Americans who see UFOs as a threat to humanity, here by the volcano at least, the opposite view was common.

The visit to Puebla and the volcano left me with much to ponder because I had yet to come across a case that featured the Tall Blondes. I had heard and read stories that such beings were from the Pleiades constellation, but my Mexican sources didn't seem to agree with that idea, so I was left with many questions about who these mysterious beings were and what they were doing here on Planet Earth. However, that was about to change in a most interesting way. Only a few months later, in October, 1995, I received a frantic call from a woman in Santa Fe, NM, named Shona, who was a 48-year-old Native American woman who worked as an artist in Santa Fe, and who had been having frightening nighttime experiences.

I sensed the same desperation, embarrassment and caution in her voice that I had heard many times before when an experiencer/abductee had called me for help. Usually by then they were desperate. The hypnotherapist is usually the last person they call, mostly because people have a natural fear of hypnosis. But who else can a person call for help? The Air Force? The police? The CIA? A doctor? A psychiatrist who knows nothing about the abduction experience? A priest or minister? None of these are good choices. Calling me was a particularly difficult choice for Shona, who had spent the first 40 years of her life in isolation on a Creek Indian reservation near Oklahoma City. Shona was a full-blooded Creek Indian, or so she thought, and came from a long line of medicine women. She herself was taught their secrets from an early age.

Shona had also been raised a Christian and had a natural fear of outsiders, particularly white men. Because of this fear, she is normally withdrawn, wary of strangers, secretive and mysterious. Immersed in the ancient knowledge and traditions of her people, she had lived a lifetime aware of the existence of other realities and spirit entities that traverse dimensional barriers. These are things she and her tribe members rarely speak about, particularly to white people, but that all changed when a series of nighttime visitations by non-human beings frightened her so badly that she became desperate for help—desperate enough to reach out to a white man.

Her first effort was to consult with a psychiatrist at a local hospital and ask him to have her placed in a psychiatric ward so she could be observed at night. As with so many other experiencers, she thought she was going crazy. However, after he heard her story, he told her he couldn't do that because he didn't think she was crazy. Amazingly, he suggested she contact the local chapter of the Mutual UFO Network (MUFON), which referred her to me, because at the time, I was a MUFON consultant and served as the assistant state director for West TX and Southern NM, and my team was conducting investigations into abduction cases.

Abruptly she said to me in a quavering voice, "I need to know what's happening to me. I need to know if I'm crazy or if this real; I need to be able to sleep at night!"

"Okay, just tell me what's been happening."

"Okay," she said, "but first I need to know if you're a Christian."

"Yes, I am," I answered.

"Good, that's important to me. I was raised a Christian on the reservation. MUFON gave me the name of someone here in Santa Fe, but I don't want to deal with anyone up here. There's too many New Age kooks here."

I had to suppress my laughter at this remark, but I finally asked her, "Why don't you just tell me what happened?"

"I've been being waked up at night by two tall white men with blue eyes and blonde hair down to their shoulders. Now I'm too scared to sleep at night. I need to know what's happening."

"Okay then, are you willing to drive the five hours down to El Paso to meet with my team?"

"Yes, I can come this weekend.'

With that, we agreed to meet Saturday afternoon at a local motel for the initial interview where she and a male friend would be staying. One of my team members went with me to meet Shona. I had already pictured what she looked like, as the El Paso area has many indigenous people. There are the Tarahumaras of northern Chihuahua to our south

Shona's drawing of a Tall Blonde   (from Author's files)

and the Mescalero Apaches in southern New Mexico. Without exception they are dark skinned and short in stature. But I was surprised when Shona came to the door.

She was very light skinned, with very high cheek bones and, although not exactly tall, she carried her statuesque body confidently erect. Nevertheless, I could tell that she was nervous and anxious to get on with the interview. She was not one to indulge in idle chatter or long introductions.

Immediately, she began telling us about her strange experiences, a conversation that I recorded. "Last summer, I went to bed and woke up at 3:33 am because the room was all lit up, real bright, but my lamp wasn't on. I looked down and saw that a part of my foot was missing. A piece about one inch deep, one inch wide, and three inches long was missing. On the inside was something silver, but there was no blood.

"Then I saw that on the left of me stood a man, and on the right of me stood a man. Both had blue eyes, with blonde hair down to their shoulders; they looked like they were about 50 years old. They were a bronze color, like they had a very good sun tan. They had on robes; one had on a white robe with gold roping around the neck, and the other had a blue robe with gold roping. The one in blue took his hand and went over my foot and my foot went back together and he said, 'Shona, you are completely healed now.' The other man bent down and put his hands on each side of my head, but he didn't touch me.

"He looked at me and said, 'We will be back when you need us.' The room stayed lit up until six that morning, and I felt I was being bathed in love."

She paused for a moment to calm herself. I was impressed at how detailed her description was of the two men and how she struggled to control her emotions. The event was still vivid in her memory, and her voice quivered as she recalled the feeling of being loved. I didn't think for a moment that she was making the story up. "Go ahead," I prompted her.

"Well, three weeks ago I woke up at about 11:30 pm and there was a man standing in my room, and he was in a white robe with white roping around the neck, blond hair down to his shoulders. He was a white man with blue eyes, and he said, 'We are giving you back your memory.' And that's all he said. He stood there all night long, and I slept on and off. Since then I have been leaving my body; it's almost like looking into the future at times. It's frightening. I became very suicidal and scared. Then they came back a week later and did some kind of surgery on me. This time it was hazy, like I had been drugged. They told me they had to fuse two disks in my back and I said, 'Why?' and one man said 'Because you need it.' He showed me a little metal thing they were going to put in my back, then they leaned me forward and I couldn't move. No marks were left, but my back was sore."

I noted that the beings could restore her memories, which I regarded as important. Controlling our memories and implanting false memories was something I had come across in my research before. For me, it was an aspect of the phenomenon that caused me to see the beings as much more than mere aliens from other planets. The beings Shona described were much more like gods or angels than aliens. Yet, as with other cases of abduction, Shona had a familiar scoop mark on her leg, indicating an implant of some type had been placed there at some time in the past. Shona had no idea when or where she had gotten it.

Shona's story was long and detailed; it involved many paranormal experiences including a near-death experience (NDE) during the birth of her daughter, due to her having Rh-negative blood, and it took the doctors a long time to find a donor. This fact also caught my attention because many abductees have Rh-negative blood. The delay caused her to leave her body, and she was pronounced dead.

"I was up on the ceiling, and I was in a warm light made of pure love. I had vision from every way you can have vision. It was amazing. I knew the secrets of the universe. Then I could feel that the doctors were tying a tag on my toe. Then, all of a sudden, I went back into my body, and it felt like I was breathing through clay because I wasn't getting enough air. Ever since then, I have been able to see what people are thinking, and I can see a person's spirit or soul floating above his head," she explained.

As with others who have had the contact experience, Shona's psychic abilities were intensified. Many find they have been given healing abilities, and some even change professions to become health workers. Although her visitations by the Tall Blondes were traumatic, they were, in fact, quite positive. During the interview, I discovered that much of the cause of her fear was due to her general fear of white men. It was due in part to her isolation on the Indian reservation for most of her life, but also because she was brutally beaten and raped as a young woman by a white man. In my mind, she was a good candidate for hypnosis. There was much more to her story, and it was time for her to recover those suppressed memories.

The following morning, as per our team protocols, I took her to meet our team psychiatrist, Dr. Roberta Fennig, who had worked with numerous abductees over the past two years. Dr. Fennig graciously donated her time to the project, and it was her job to conduct a psychiatric evaluation before we could conclude that Shona was a suitable subject for hypnosis. Early on, we had decided to weed out those who were unstable or on too many medications to qualify for our study. Dr. Fennig's recommendation was this:

"Shona does not suffer from any mental illness, and she is not hallucinating. The visions she describes are too real, consistent, and detailed to be hallucinations. Shona questions her own sanity and the reality of what she is seeing with a lot of conflict and emotion. Shona functions normally in all other areas of her life. Her ego and self-image are strong, but when she tries to fit these unusual events into her everyday life, she experiences a feeling of conflict, which produces severe anxiety and fear. Regressive hypnotherapy can help her make the connection between the two different realities, thereby reducing the conflict."

We proceeded with the hypnosis, which I would normally have performed, but there was a problem. I was a white man, and Shona was not comfortable with white men. So, Dr. Fennig conducted the session, and Shona was able to go into a deep trance quite easily. Below is a condensed portion of the session. For more information about Shona's case, the reader may wish to acquire a copy of *The God Hypothesis,* which gives the complete version of her case.

Dr. Fennig began by asking about the first time the Tall Blondes visited her in Santa Fe. Shona began to sob and shake as she recalled the scene. "They healed my foot.... They have great power, and they want me to know."

Dr. Roberta Fennig (RF): Is this a lesson for you?

Shona (S): I know it.

RF: How do you know it?

S: Because they gave it to me when I was born.... They were there.

RF: Can you go back to a time when you first knew these beings?

S: They have always been here.

RF: Can you ask them what their purpose is?

S: They're here to help. They don't live here.

RF: Where do they live?

S: Another place. It's pretty there. The air is good, and there is no disease, and it's never dark.

RF: Have you been there?

S: (Choking back tears) Yes, I was a boy (crying). When I lived there, I was a boy. (Deep sobs and moans) They want me to go to Earth. I don't want to go.

RF: Why did they send you here?

S: To help.... He's my daddy...the one in the red.... I like him.

RF: Do you know what they call the place they come from?

S: It has two suns.... There's trees and rivers.

RF: And how do they get from that place to this place?

S: They come in ships.

RF: Have you ever been on those ships?

S: Yes, last week.

RF: Who do you see on those ships?

S: They're all blonde headed with blue eyes. Some wear robes, some wear uniforms.... My father and his father...they sent me here. But when I woke up, I wasn't five.... I was a baby....They brought me here in a tube.... I want to go home! (tearfully) They say I have to stay....They're coming here. They're coming to take a lot of the people away.

RF: Why are they taking them?

S: This world is no good. It's no good to live here.

RF: When they said they would give you back your memories, what did that mean?

S: I can remember my home.... I have to learn how to help the people of Earth. They don't understand what they're doing. They're destroying everything.... They don't care.

RF: What is the difference between the blonde beings and what people call angels?

S: There is no difference.

RF: Is there anything you can tell us about Jesus?

S: He flies in ships too. He lives on another world... the first world.... He came here, like me, in a tube, like a pill...a capsule.

After the hypnosis session, when Shona was fully awake, her perceptions of reality were shaken to the core. As a Christian, she had never believed in reincarnation, yet she could not deny her vivid memories and the strong emotions that came with them. And the idea that Jesus flies in a spaceship and was brought here in a capsule, possibly an embryo that was implanted in a woman, as she had been, was also a cause of great dissonance and certainly contrary to what she was taught as a Christian. Now fully awake, she began to question what she said under hypnosis. She thought she might have made it all up. "Where did that come from?" she wondered. She was also greatly disturbed by the notion that she was actually half white, and had been a white boy in a past life.

Her skepticism caused her to question the hypnosis process altogether, and she insisted on coming back in the afternoon for a second session to test her memories. Dr. Fennig agreed to give up her afternoon for another session during which Shona confirmed that her memories were correct. At last, she was convinced that she had found her soul connection to the race of Tall Blondes—and that changed her life.

After Shona returned to Santa Fe, I was left pondering the remarkable coincidence that she had come to me shortly after my trip to Mexico. I began to think that there might be another reason for showing up just after my introductions to the Tall Blondes during my trip to Puebla. Perhaps Shona was sent to me by the Blondes as a lesson to teach me as well. Maybe it was not a coincidence at all, but a synchronous event orchestrated by these higher beings. I began to realize that the odd things that happened to me might have been orchestrated as well. I had to admit, my life has always been full of synchronicities.

17

Confirmation

To say that Dr. Fennig and I were amazed at the information that Shona's Tall Blondes revealed to her is an understatement. We were confident that Shona was being truthful and that her Tall Blondes were not figments of her imagination. We were also certain that the beings were conveying important information to her and to us. Up to that point we had investigated more than two dozen cases of abduction and we had attended workshops given by Dr. Mack and by MUFON's director of abduction research, John Carpenter. We knew all the subtle clues that indicated a true case versus one that just didn't add up. Shona's case added up in all of those ways.

We marveled at how our investigation into the phenomenon had taken a sharp turn away from the prevailing view that aliens from other planets were here to take over the Earth (the ET hypothesis). Other mainstream researchers were not discussing reincarnation and past lives, but we had seemingly been steered toward that connection from the start of our research.

We wondered if it was possible that other researchers had such cases, but were concealing them. Perhaps they had cast the information aside and deleted it from their files because they deemed it unimportant or too controversial.

Or, maybe reincarnation and spirituality did not fit into their atheistic or agnostic world views.

Whatever the case, our team had the concept of past lives thrust into our research from almost our first case. A Mexican-American woman in her early 40s, whom I refer to as Alicia, came to us for help because her son was having night terrors and her family was frightened by poltergeist activity in their home, another aspect of the phenomenon not usually reported by the mainstream. In her very first hypnosis session, conducted by El Paso Community College sociology professor Dr. Romeo Di Benedetto, who owned the Southwest Hypnotherapy Clinic, Alicia began speaking in French, a language she did not speak in her present life.

Dr. Di Benedetto, a masterful hypnotherapist, had been a Catholic priest in his early life, but had left the Church to marry and raise a family many years before. He was able to coax Alicia into speaking in English (with a thick French accent) so we could understand her. It turned out that she was reliving a past life in the outskirts of Paris in the 1700s where her father practiced medicine and she worked as a spiritual healer, very much as she did in this life.

Alicia worked at a hospital as a speech therapist, but she was using her healing ability secretly to help her patients. She got such good results that word spread around the hospital, and she was often called in on an unofficial basis to help with all kinds of difficult cases. Without making a big deal of it, the doctors and nurses knew that Alicia had special healing powers that did not conform to modern medical practices. She was a miracle worker. She was also an abductee.

Under hypnosis, when I asked her how she learned to be a healer in her past life in France, she began to speak about a spiritual master who was her teacher in yet another past life, many ages before. She recalled being with him and his followers on the side of a hill where many hundreds of people were seated to hear the master speak.

"I was given a basket full of loaves of bread, covered by a cloth, and I was told to feed the people," she remembered. "How can I feed so many people?" she cried. But as she passed among the people passing out loaves of bread, something very strange happened. "The basket is staying full. It never runs out of bread!" she said, in astonishment. Then, after the master spoke, she found herself standing next to him, and with tears streaming down her cheeks, and holding her hands in the air as if to grasp something, she said, "I'm holding his face in my hands!"

After the hypnosis, which also revealed that she, in this life, was involved as a surrogate mother in the alien hybrid-baby program, Alicia experienced tremendous emotional conflict. In the debriefing, when she was asked who this master was, she would look down at the floor and repeat the word, "conflict, conflict, conflict." Finally, I just asked her if it was Jesus. After a long moment of reflection, Alicia tearfully admitted that the master who was speaking and who was her spiritual teacher was, in fact, Jesus. One might wonder why it was so difficult for her to name Jesus as the master. The answer was that Alicia is Jewish.

Any Christian knows that what Alicia described under hypnosis is the story of The Sermon on the Mount, as told in *Matthew* chapters 5-7. In his sermon, Jesus teaches the people how to live a Godly life despite all the difficulties the world faces. In the end, he teaches the throng to pray, by reciting the Lord's Prayer, known to Christians around the world today. All the while, as he speaks, his disciples are feeding the people fish and bread from baskets that never empty. Alicia then, was recalling a past life as a disciple of Jesus, which was a shocking revelation to Alicia, who as a Jewish woman in her current life, had denied Jesus's standing as the Jewish Messiah and the Son of God, as Christians believe.

This case was another example of a person who remembered a powerful and emotional past life that totally contradicted her current beliefs, just as in Shona's case.

But why, I wondered, if past-life memories are nothing but fantasies, as many people believe, would a person come up with a fantasy that totally contradicted their most closely held beliefs in their current lives? I can't imagine a reason why that would happen. In fact, such contradictions actually make a strong argument for the validity of hypnotherapy and the memories that it elicits.

18

The Cosmic Game Wardens

Throughout time humans have struggled to attach a name to the beings who hover over us and rule our world behind a veil of secrecy. But we must call them something. We sometimes settle for calling them aliens (as I do) simply because they seem different from us, and it simplifies the matter, but some would rather not use that term because it inevitably associates them with UFOs and the accompanying ridicule that goes with it. One such person is the late Englishman and Nobel Laureate, Francis Crick, who, with American James Watson, discovered the double-helix structure of the DNA molecule in 1953.

Crick became quite uneasy about the complexity of the amazing molecule that morphs itself into every living thing, from an oak tree to a human. He began to contemplate how such a thing could have come into being. It seemed too complex to have just sprung up by chance in a

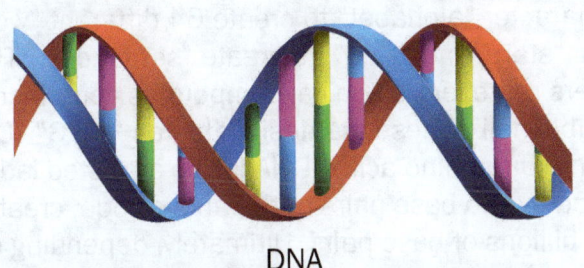

DNA

Francis Crick, co-discoverer of DNA,
admitted to having used LSD to help him visualize
its double-helix structure.

primordial ocean, as mainstream scientists had concluded. There is just something strange going on here, he thought. The more we know about it, the more alien it appears.

The DNA molecule is a microscopic, self-replicating "machine," which, by rearranging the letters in its mysterious code, is responsible for the diversity of all life on Planet Earth. At the molecular level there is no difference between a leaf and a human. This uniformity found in every cell in every living thing was shocking. For a species that prides itself on its individuality and superiority over all other life forms, this finding was not welcome. It just didn't compute.

To fully understand this dilemma, one must understand just how complex this tiny machine is. Firstly, it uses a four-character "alphabet" to create 64 different "words", including "start" and "stop", to create "sentences." These four letters represent chemical compounds contained in the DNA double helix. These are designated as "A" "G" "C" and "T," for the four amino acids. DNA is like a twisted ladder connected by two base pairs of the above code, creating a string of billions of base pairs. Ultimately, depending on how these letters are arranged, it can create anything from an orchid to a human. The human code includes more than two billion base pairs.

But there is more to the story. For DNA to replicate, it must use yet another "alphabet" of 20 letters—proteins. The problem here is that the much-more-complex protein "language" must be able to communicate with the simpler four-letter "language." It's like going to a foreign country and trying to speak to people whose language you don't know. Obviously, you need a translator, just as DNA does. Amazingly, there are translators built into the DNA molecule. These translators are chemicals called enzymes.

When biologists speak about the DNA molecule they talk about it as if it were a factory in which two languages are spoken, and in which translators are needed so that "robots" can put everything in order so the molecule can replicate itself. Crick was astonished at this complexity and began to try to determine if such a molecule could simply have sprung up spontaneously, through billions of years of evolution, or if something else was going on. His conclusion was that it was simply not possible for it to have evolved naturally on Earth or anywhere else. *This conclusion, obviously, created a problem. If DNA didn't evolve on its own, then it was brought or sent here from somewhere else, and someone must have made it.*

In his 1981 *Life Itself: Its Nature and Origins*, Crick speculates on the origins of the DNA molecule, expanding on a theory that he first developed in the 1970s together with Leslie Orgel, a pioneer in prebiotic chemistry. Crick writes that DNA was either brought here by space-faring extraterrestrials, or that it was seeded here through the use of robotic spacecraft by some distant, advanced civilization. Crick called his theory "Directed Panspermia." The notion that DNA arrived here from outer space was originally proposed by Swedish chemist and Nobel laureate Svante Arrhenius, at the turn of the 20th century. He called his theory "Panspermia," which proposed that DNA arrived here in meteorites. Crick didn't believe the molecule could have survived on the back of a rock hurling through our atmosphere, so the theory required someone directing it purposefully toward Earth. (More recently, science has accepted that it is possible for such a molecule to have arrived inside a comet or rocky meteorite.)

Crick arrived at his conclusion after conducting a sophisticated computer analysis to calculate the odds that a complex molecule could have been formed by accident, such as a chemical reaction caused by a lightning bolt striking a primordial ocean. He discovered that the odds were so outrageously against such an occurrence that he ruled it impossible. His calculations showed that the odds of that happening were greater than the number of all the atoms in the universe! He basically debunked the idea that it evolved over billions of years, as evolutionists proclaim. That argument, he believed, is flawed because there is no evidence for an evolutionary process that gradually creates molecules by trial and error. For example, ancient fossilized bacteria, billions of years old, are no different than today's bacteria. All ancient DNA discovered in fossils is the same as the DNA of today.

After discarding an accidental creation or an evolutionary development of DNA, Crick was left with only one solution: Someone with sublime intelligence must have made the molecule and then directed it toward us. The other obvious choice would have been that God created it, but that would have put Crick in the uncomfortable position of being drawn into a religious debate, on the side of creationists, who dispute the whole idea of evolution. To defend against the inevitable ridicule from the scientific world, Crick fought vigorously to disavow any perceived connection between his theory and any modern-day UFO theories that might be similar. Crick writes, "The whole idea stinks of UFOs or *The Chariots of the Gods*, or other common forms of contemporary silliness. Against this, I can only claim that whereas the idea has indeed many of the stigmata of science fiction, its body is a lot more solid. It does not really have the major features of most science fiction, which is a great leap of the imagination.... Each of the details which contribute to the required scenario are based on a fairly solid foundation of contemporary science." (Crick, 1981, p. 149.)

Struggling to steer away from what he called "silliness" of UFO terminology, Crick chose not to call these advanced beings "aliens." *He proposed a new term by speculating that whoever brought or sent DNA here might view life on Earth as an experiment*, returning from time to time to see how things are going. He suggested that Planet Earth might be a giant wildlife preserve, presided over by what he called, "Cosmic Game Wardens." Crick wrote: "Perhaps we are under some sort of discreet surveillance by higher beings on a planet of a nearby star. It is not clear exactly how these cosmic game wardens would do this without our detecting them, but with a higher technology such supervision may be relatively easy."

19

The Custodians

Author and hypnotist Dolores Cannon (1931-2014) was raised as a Christian in St. Louis, MO, where she lived for the first 20 years of her pretty-much ordinary life. But that changed when, at 20, she married a Navy man, had children, and spent the next 20 years broadening her horizons by following him all over the world. Her first exposure to hypnosis and the concept of reincarnation came in 1968 when her husband, also an amateur hypnotist, stumbled on a past life while working with a woman who had a weight problem.

Many Christians in that situation, and at that time, would have thought it was the work of the Devil and steered clear of the whole issue, but Dolores had a powerful sense of curiosity that caused her to overcome her religious upbringing and decide to learn more about hypnosis and past-life memories. In 1970, after the couple retired and moved to Arkansas, and when her children were grown, she began a career as a writer and looked further into the study of hypnosis by reading everything she could find on the subject. As a self-taught hypnotist, she began helping people with their ordinary problems such as losing weight and ceasing bad habits like smoking. But she also began helping them remember their past lives. That was her focus and her passion for nearly a decade, but that changed in 1985 when a friend invited her to attend a meeting with members of the Mutual UFO Network (MUFON), and she was introduced to the work being done to investigate UFO sightings and abductions. "My friend knew about my interest in the strange and unusual and thought I might like to meet some of the investigators," she wrote in the introduction to her 1999 *The Custodians: Beyond Abduction*. Shortly after that MUFON meeting, she began to work with abductees, learning about the bizarre beings behind this strange phenomenon. By 1999 she had carefully recorded and cataloged several hundred cases of regressive hypnosis including both past-life memories and those of alien encounters. In her many books, she published entire transcripts of those hypnosis sessions, something no other researchers were doing at the time.

She describes her first abduction case as: "being introduced into the world of the little gray beings who removed people from their homes at night, tests performed on-board spacecraft, star maps, and encounters tracing back to childhood. It was also my first exposure to the fear and trauma felt by the subject. These feelings were so prevalent that the emotion blocked the obtaining of information.... The (subject) could not find answers to the many questions I asked." Dolores, as had other researchers, had to find a way to break through the barrier.

Eventually, she was able to calm the fears and find the answers the subject was looking for, but at first, she was just overwhelmed by the phenomenon she had stumbled into. Her first case opened the door to working with other cases; she was able to discern a pattern that included being taken by the little gray beings with large eyes, and having various tests performed. Sometimes, other, more human-looking beings, were reported, as well as strange, insect-like beings that looked like giant praying mantises. As with other researchers, she gradually began to recognize the common scenario that included a round or curved room, an operating table, a bright light above the subject, strange medical instruments and computer-like machines. Many reported their first experience as having occurred in childhood. Some cases, in which other family members were involved, seemed like a generational study, in which grandparents, parents, children and grandchildren were all part of a long-term investigation. They all seemed to have been monitored throughout their lives.

She learned from the beings themselves that they had been watching life on Earth since its very beginnings. She began to realize that they had been monitoring our development covertly in a way that their subjects' lives would not be affected. These revelations prodded her to write *Keepers of the Garden* in 1993, which revealed that the beings are greatly concerned with chemicals and pollutants in the atmosphere, and that drugs, medications and alcohol were damaging the brains of all humans. This was part of the reason for the regular testing during abduction experiences. As a credit to her, she did not conclude that the beings were evil or even a threat to humanity, as some other researchers had. Very soon, she began to see the phenomenon as critical to human existence and to our understanding of who we humans are.

"I have discovered glimpses of a much bigger picture that is only now beginning to surface: a picture which our human minds can barely comprehend. It could be the biggest picture ever shown to humanity: the story of who we are, where we came from, and where we are going."

She even concluded that their genetic manipulation program, in which they create human/alien hybrids, was not a threat to the human race, as other researchers had concluded, but rather a benign and necessary endeavor:

"My theories are different. I do not believe they are doing this for their purposes, but for ours. Of course, we have seen that there are several different types of entities involved, and there could be some negative types doing these things for their own gains. But I believe these are in the minority....There is a higher power at work directing a plan that was fashioned for our world eons before the first human appeared upon our planet....The beings were assigned the carrying out of various steps in this project.... As they produced life on our planet, nurtured it and pruned it over eons of time, it was only a job, an assignment. They may have had similar assignments on various other planets at various stages of its growth...."

It's easy to see that Dolores's conclusions coincide neatly with Francis Crick's theory of Directed Panspermia and his naming of the beings who seeded life on Earth as "Cosmic Game Wardens." Dolores's use of the terms "Custodians" and "Keepers of the Garden" are precisely what Crick alluded to in his 1981 *Life Itself*. What is amazing is that they both reached the same conclusion through different means—Crick, through the use of the scientific method and Dolores, through the use of a patently unscientific method—hypnosis.

A Gray alien drawn by Karen Pennison, one of Dolores Cannon's hypnosis subjects, from *The Custodians*.

20

Jesus and the Essenes

Dolores Cannon was a fearless researcher who didn't hold back from reporting on her findings, no matter how strange or distant they were from mainstream scientific and religious beliefs. She didn't worry about what her critics or the scientific community would say about her books, or how those opinions might affect her book sales. She was retired and not beholding to an employer who might be embarrassed by what she wrote. (As I was.) She sold her books at New Age and UFO conferences, where she was many times the keynote speaker. Her message was getting through, and she had a large following of devotees.

So, when she found a hypnosis subject who remembered a life as an Essene teacher of Jesus, her natural inclination was to write another book focusing on the story of Jesus. But then she had second thoughts. In her 1992 *Jesus and the Essenes: Fresh Insights into Christ's Ministry and the Dead Sea Scrolls*, she hesitated. "I was...reluctant to tell anyone that I had discovered someone who was one of the Essene teachers of Jesus. I was sure I would get a smirk of disbelief and some snide remark, such as, "Oh, yeah? Now tell me another," as though I thought them gullible enough to swallow anything. I can understand that. I am sure I would have been skeptical if I had heard this from someone else."

Yet she was certain the information was valid; she had been working with a woman whom she called "Katie" for almost a year on a weekly basis and had uncovered 26 past lives almost equally divided between male and female, rich and poor, intelligent and uneducated. In none of these did she remember being anyone famous: "Each [was] filled with a wealth of detail about the religious dogma and cultural customs of the time period. I am positive even a scholar trained in history and anthropology could not come up with the incredible detail that she gave us."

What made this case even more credible was the fact that Katie kept coming up with information that contradicted her religious beliefs and the Bible itself. In her current life, Katie had been raised in a family of devout members of the Assembly of God Church—a rigid Christian sect that believes that the Bible is the inerrant word of God, a sect in which no one teaches about or believes in reincarnation.

Katie was only 22, a bit immature, and certainly not knowledgeable about ancient Judaism, the Dead Sea Scrolls or the Essenes. But she was adventurous and curious enough to volunteer as a subject of Dolores's past-life regression study. She was one who could enter a deep, somnambulistic trance state, recover detailed memories of past lives, but not be able to recall what she said under hypnosis. After working with Katie for almost nine months, Dolores took her back to a 27th past life and what emerged was stunning. Katie began speaking in a deep masculine voice with a strong accent who identified himself as "Suddi." He said he was walking to the town of Nazareth to see his cousins, and that it was located in Galilee. He said he was 30 and not married. He described his home in the hills above a community he called "Kum-a-ran" and that his occupation included studying the Torah, "I study the law, Hebrew law," he said.

Still, Dolores was not connecting the dots. At the time, she knew almost nothing of the Essenes, the Dead Sea Scrolls, a place called Qumran, or Judaism in general:

The ruins at Qumran. The long room, where the scrolls were thought to be written and copied, was called the "scriptorium."

"As a Protestant, I didn't know what the Torah was, and I thought he meant law such as legal law that is used in courts. I was to receive much education within the next few months as I discovered the Torah was the Jewish religious book, and the law referred to the laws of Moses, which Jewish people pattern their lives after.... I have had little contact with Jewish people, know almost nothing about the Jewish religion, and had never been to a synagogue."

This put her at a great disadvantage, because the therapist must know what questions to ask her subject. Hypnotizing a person is relatively easy, but knowing the questions to ask and how to ask them is crucial. In this case, Dolores was feeling her way around like a blind person, asking simple questions and hoping to learn who this man was by his answers. As she explained, "When I am working with Katie, I often feel very stupid, because I do not know the basic things about the time period she is in.... I often feel I am only going along for the ride."

Soon, it was established that Suddi was training to be a teacher and that he had masters who taught him. "Who are your masters?" she asked, and he named his teachers of mathematics, of the mysteries, and of the Torah. Then, he said something quite interesting. "My teacher of righteousness is (name unclear). She teaches the things that have been handed down, all of the laws of truth, of things that are protected."

Here, Suddi uses the term "Teacher of Righteousness," which we know from the Scrolls was the Essene leader of the community at Qumran. Clearly, at the time when Suddi was a student, the title was assigned to a woman, which was quite extraordinary, yet not mentioned in the Scrolls, as they only refer to their members by their titles, so as to keep their identities hidden. But this woman who bore the title, it turns out, held the title before Jesus, who arrived at the community years later, as a child. Dolores, grasping at straws, asked Suddi, "Hasn't it been said that the Messiah has already come?"

"No, he has not come, for the heavens have not let it be known. It is said that from four corners stars will rise together and when they meet it will be the time of His birth."

She asked him if he knew of a man named Jesus (an inappropriately leading question if there ever was one), but, pushing back, he said he knew no one by that name in Nazareth. Then she asked if Bethlehem was near, and he said it was. "I've also heard of the country Judaea. Is that near here?" she asked.

"It is here," he answered emphatically.

Finally, having established where this lifetime took place, Dolores asked a good follow-up question, "Who is the ruler at this time in your land?"

"King Herod," he answered.

Dolores now understood the importance of this man's life. "I felt a shiver of excitement. Maybe Jesus had not been born yet." She then asked: "Have you ever heard of a group that is known as the Essenes?"

Suddi responded, "They are my teachers."

Dolores: "I have heard they are like a secret organization, would that be correct?"

"They are greatly feared by those who are in power, because we have studied into the mysteries that others have only hinted at, and they fear that if we gain too much power and knowledge that they will lose their place."

Dolores: "How do they differ from the regular Jewish community?

Suddi: "There is more strict adherence to the laws.... Much time is spent upon the defining of the prophecies given. And knowing that this is the time that they shall be culminated...it is our duty to prepare others for this time, and to prepare the way."

Dolores asked if there was a name for their kind of religion, and Suddi answered, "It has no name; we are known as the Essenes.... It is a school of thought, not a religion.... We believe in God the father, Yahweh. It means, 'with no name,' for God is the nameless one, he has no name that man has knowledge of. They are also known as the Elohim and Eloi, they are basically the same thing."

Although Dolores and her team did not understand the significance of these words, they later discovered that the terms "Elohim and Eloi" are plural forms of the word "El," a primitive, generic term meaning God that is used in Semitic languages. To the Canaanites, the God "El" was an immoral and debased character, but when the Hebrews took over the term, it lost its evil connotation. (See *The Compact Bible Dictionary* for more on this subject.)

Thus, the Elohim are angelic beings who are God's representatives on Earth. In some UFO abduction cases, the Tall Blondes identify themselves as the Elohim. (See Dana Redfield's 1999 autobiographical book about her encounters, *Summoned: Encounters with Alien Intelligence*, as an example.) It is also important to note that the idea that God has no name, or that it should never be spoken, is a notion used by Jesus when he delivers the Sermon on the Mount and teaches the people what we know as the Lord's Prayer: "Our Father who art in heaven, hallowed be thy name..." Here we see that Jesus, as a true Essene who adheres to strict Jewish law, teaches the throng that God's name is sacred and should not be uttered.

Dolores's method was to gradually move the subject's past-life memories forward in time. When the life of Suddi, the Essene, was discovered, he was 30 and still a student living in the hills above Qumran. Jesus had not yet been born, so Suddi did not recognize his name. But he explained that the Essenes were anxiously expecting the Messiah to be born soon. Before getting to the time when Suddi would become an Essene teacher, he gave Dolores some very interesting information that her hypnosis subject, Katie, would not likely have known. Regarding the Bible story of Ezekiel, Suddi explained that he had been visited by some of the "others," and he had been taken away.

Dolores pushed him to explain who the "others" were. Suddi explained: "There are others similar to us, but not the same.... They are not of Earth, they are from elsewhere.... We are told that as far back as there is remembrance, there have been visitors.... Some (people) are visited, some are again taken away, but some are left here to speak of the experience.... I believe they used the term 'chariots of fire.' But it was more like one of the flying machines of old [than] a chariot."

Later, speaking of the origins of the human race, he said the angelic beings created life on Earth and experimented over the eons to create the best life-form. Then, souls, described as "little sparks" of the whole (God) incarnated into human bodies to experience what life on Earth would be like. At first the souls could come and go at will, but the longer they stayed, the more "warped" the souls became, thus becoming trapped.

Dolores later asked if the community had ever had contact with beings from another world or planet. Suddi answered: "Yes.... It is those of the Watchers who guard what we do. They are pleased in our efforts to keep the knowledge, to bring about the peace."

It is doubtful that Katie would have known much about the Watchers, as they are mentioned only briefly in the Torah and in today's Bible. However, the Essenes revered the Books of Enoch, which speak at length about the Watchers, and were found in abundance among the Dead Sea Scrolls. Therefore, Suddi would have been knowledgeable on the subject.

Moving on to the prophecy of a coming Messiah, Suddi explained that "He shall be of the house of David" and would be born in Bethlehem. "It is said that the time is soon, very soon."

"Will he be born or will he just appear?"

"He shall be born of a woman," Suddi replied.... It is said that Elias (Elijah) shall have to come before to pave the way."

"What do you mean?"

"He shall be reborn. He is to pave the way. To let those who know who are listening that the Messiah comes."

Dolores: "Do you know who he will be reborn as?"

"I do not know." (Of course he is referring to John the Baptist, according to the Bible.)

"What about the Messiah, is he going to be the rebirth of someone else?"

Seeming uncertain or deceptive, Suddi responds, "He is Moses or Adam, it is the same." The name of the Messiah, as we now know, was Yeshua/Joshua/Jesus, the reincarnation of the prophet "Joshua," but that name would have been a well-kept secret among the Essenes.

Moving Suddi forward in that lifetime, Dolores arrives at the moment of the Messiah's birth, which occurs when four strange "stars" come together in the sky above Bethlehem and shoot down a beam of light, which can be seen from Qumran.

"Has Elias also come again?" Dolores asks.

"He has been born also. It was a few months before. His father is known to us, for he is of us." (Although the Bible doesn't identify the father of John the Baptist, Zachariah, as an Essene, it can be deduced from the story of John the Baptist that he most likely was.) It describes John as having been raised in the wilderness, meaning the Judean desert, where Qumran is located. John would have been known as the son of Zachariah, or, "Ben-Zachariah."

As for the Messiah, Suddi says, "His mother was but a child.... The father was older, a very pious man.... They had been together many times before in other lives." Then he explains that the Messiah had been brought to Qumran for protection when he was just a baby, just as John had been. As the children grew, Suddi became obsessed with protecting them from danger. Describing the two as they got older, Suddi said that John was "fierce as a lion. He is strong and lets everyone know exactly what he is thinking.... He looks much like his cousin (Jesus)." But he described Jesus as being "calmer and finer."

As Dolores moved Suddi forward in that lifetime, she finds him teaching two students at Qumran. "I teach the law. This seems to me very odd. How can one teach the law to someone who knows it better than I know it myself?"

"Are you speaking of your students?"

"I am speaking of one of them, yes."

Dolores asks for an example of something the student has taught him. Suddi explains how this one student, whom he won't name, is very observant and finds deep meaning in the natural world, meaning that can be used to teach people about their own existence. One lesson is about reincarnation, or as he put it, "the cycles of life." It is about how plants grow and put out their seeds, which then spring back up to new life. "The plant putting up new plants from the roots was like a man going through rebirths... and starts new families."

Another example was when the student compares the waves of the sea that pick up bits of debris and moves them forward. The student said, "You go through your cycle of life, starting at one point and then, when you die, it's like being picked up by a wave and then being redeposited in another life.... Your spirit is redeposited, and it's a little further along the way of where you're meaning to go."

But still, Suddi would not reveal the names of his students, so Dolores pushed a little harder to find out. Suddi finally answered, using surnames only: "There is young Ben-Joseph and then there is Ben-Zachariah."

He was not aware, Dolores thought, that these names were enough for her to identify them. But now she was sure his students were John the Baptist and Jesus.

As Suddi's life progressed, he tells how his students "graduated" and were given certificates at the age of 14 to show that they had successfully gained sufficient knowledge of the Law to be considered "First in Law."

As time goes by, Jesus leaves to travel to other countries, but returns to Qumran for further teaching. Suddi grows old and leaves to live with family in Nazareth. By then, Jesus has begun his ministry, and Suddi has no reason to continue protecting his name. Dolores says, "I thought perhaps now Suddi would tell me Ben-Joseph's other name."

Suddi: "Yeshua, this is his name."

The story of Suddi and the Essenes as told in Dolores Cannon's book is a lengthy one and requires us to ask ourselves a number of questions.

First, it is fair to ask an important question about Dolores. How credible is she? My answer is that even though she was not certified as a hypnotherapist and is a self-taught hypnotist, I believe that she is honestly concerned for her subject's welfare. Despite the fact that she had very little knowledge of the time during which Suddi lived, and that she asked far too many leading questions, she was able to retrieve much historically accurate information without causing her subject any harm. Some hypnotists would push a subject to provide answers that they were more comfortable with—more in line with their own religious beliefs. I don't think this is the case in the present situation.

Secondly, how accurate is the information provided by Katie's subconscious (or higher consciousness as I prefer to call it)? As a long-time and experienced hypnotherapist who has been certified in past-life regression therapy by the American Board of Hypnotherapy, I can say that a great deal of it is accurate. I also bring much additional expertise to the discussion, as I have studied in great depth the ancient Scrolls, the Lost Gospels and the Bible. However, we also must consider the fact that while a person may be in a very deep trance, her conscious mind may still be skewing some of the information being brought forward. It's very hard to say if this happened in this case, because we don't know much about Katie's religious beliefs before her hypnosis.

In this case, Katie is very young and certainly is not an expert in any of the extra-Biblical areas by any means. It is highly doubtful that she was familiar with the Books of Enoch or the Dead Sea Scrolls, for example. Additionally, just as we have seen in the previously mentioned cases of Shona and Alicia, Katie is recalling a great deal of information regarding the cycle of life and reincarnation. Katie would not have known that the ancient Hebrews believed that their patriarchs were the reincarnations of other past leaders, as Jewish historian Josephus Flavius wrote about in his history of the Jewish people 2,000 years ago. For these reasons, I felt that it was important to include Dolores's powerful case study in this book.

21

A Purposeful Universe

Do we live in an accidental universe, one in which everything happens randomly? Or do we live in a purposeful universe in which our lives are scripted before we're born, and unseen forces arrange "coincidental" events that lead us in preordained directions? I believe that if we examine our lives carefully, we will find "coincidences" that are too strange to be accidental. Such events are called "synchronicities," and are full of meaning. Sometimes they can even be seen as miracles. Interestingly, I am not the only one who has noticed this. Albert Einstein said, "There are two kinds of people in the world, those who do not believe in miracles, and those who believe that miracles happen every day. I believe in the latter." So, if miracles happen every day, why don't we notice them? Perhaps we're just not looking. Is it possible that something as common as falling in love has already been determined by a higher power?

Oftentimes, finding a life partner entails a number of "coincidences" that lead to an unexpected meeting. For example, my wife (Hilda) and I married when she was 28 and I was 29. We had known each other in high school, but then we went our separate ways. I was finishing my Ph.D. work at the University of Missouri, and she was living in Houston working as a school teacher. Neither of us were on the other's radar, yet we both decided to move back to our home town of El Paso temporarily at about the same time. I returned to El Paso to finish writing my dissertation, but I was planning to take a job I was offered in Washington, D.C., at the Department of Justice soon after. I was under pressure from my advisory committee to finish my manuscript, which had been bought by a big New York publishing company that was also anxious to see the completed work.

She, on the other hand, had tired of teaching seventh graders and was looking about for something else to do. Ultimately, she decided to move to San Francisco to live with her older sister and seek a job there. She decided to make a temporary stop in El Paso, stay with her parents for the summer, and take a photography course at the University. So, we both arrived at about the same time. Then something quite out of the blue happened. I was offered to chair the journalism department at the University of Texas at El Paso, and I decided to take it and not return to Washington. Coincidentally, the photography course she was taking was part of my department. We met in the hallway by my office, which she had to pass to get to her class.

In short, our first date was in October, we were engaged in December, and we were married in March. In 2025 we celebrated our 51st wedding anniversary. A long time after we were married, she told me that a psychic had told her in Houston that we were going to meet. Naturally, I was skeptical. "No, really," she explained. "I went with a friend to have our fortunes told by a young woman who we heard was amazing. She laid out the Tarot cards on the table, and she told me that I would be moving west soon, and that I would meet my husband, who was now living in the Midwest, and that he would be a doctor, not a medical doctor, but a Ph.D. She also said he would have dark hair."

She could see that I was still not receptive to the idea that a psychic had foretold our meeting and marriage, so she said, "Do you want to hear the tape?"

"The tape? What tape?"

"I recorded the reading, and I still have the tape. I never listened to it, but I still have it. Do you want to hear it?"

"Sure," I said, still not believing.

Within a few minutes she found the tape and played it on her little tape recorder. What we heard shocked both of us. We could clearly hear the psychic tell her fortune exactly as she remembered. She foretold that she would move west (at the time she had not made any plans or had any thought of leaving Houston.) The psychic said that she would meet her husband, who was, at that time, in the Midwest, and that he would have dark hair and would be a doctor. Then she paused and corrected herself. "No, he's not a doctor of medicine. He's a Ph.D." That part that gave me chills.

It made me think, "Is it possible that we are not the captains of our own ships, that our lives are already planned out for us before we're born? Is someone up above watching us and orchestrating our lives to make sure the plan is carried out? Do we live in a purposeful universe?"

On the one hand, I was shocked, but the fact was that I had already experienced an amazing "coincidence" that saved my life—a very strange one. It happened in 1967 when I was in the Army in Vietnam. I was an aviator assigned to a reconnaissance company in the Central Highlands, an area covered with high mountains and triple-canopy jungle foliage. Our reconnaissance planes were little, single-engine Cessnas. They had a two-seater cabin, so an observer could sit in the back, but often we would fly alone, barely above the trees at just under 100 mph. We were sitting ducks that the enemy loved to use for shooting practice. Some of them were very good shots, as I quickly found out.

One day I was on patrol near the Cambodian border when I got caught up in a fast-moving storm and had no choice but to go in one direction—up. Our planes were not meant to be flown through the clouds, even though we had been thoroughly trained to fly on instruments. Soon, I found myself above the clouds at 10,000 feet, with no way down.

The clouds extended as far as I could see, and I realized this was no little storm, but a dreaded monsoon. I couldn't fly down again through the clouds because of the mountains, and if I flew far enough to the east, I would have to deal with the South China Sea. That sounded better, but still, the clouds went almost down to the ground and there might not be enough space between the two to pull up and avoid slamming into the sea. I was in a real predicament. To make matters worse, my radio informed me that all the airfields were closed, which eliminated the possibility of being vectored in for an instrument landing by a ground controller at an Air Force base, who could watch me on radar.

The only thing I could do was head due east and rely on my instruments to let me know about when I was crossing over the shore. Maybe there would be a break in the clouds somewhere out there. I knew I had to go down sometime, when I ran out of fuel. The "coincidence" happened just as I deduced that the shoreline was near. Scanning the cloud layer to my right, I saw something odd—it looked like a hole in the clouds. I flew over to look at it and it was indeed a hole—a perfect, cookie-cutter round one that went 10,000 feet straight down. It was just big enough to fit a small airplane in a tight spin. I could see, way below me, waves pounding on the beach, exactly where I needed to be!

Even though I knew such things just don't happen, I didn't hesitate. I put the plane in a tight spin and spun all the way down, hoping the hole would hold its shape. Miraculously it did, but as soon as I was down, I turned my plane around so I could look at the hole one last time, only to see it close up and disappear. Things like that just shouldn't happen. But it happened to me. All I could think was "Somebody up there must like me!"

I think this was the first time that I realized that there are no coincidences, and that I had guardian angels looking over me and guiding my life. I began to pay attention to other meaningful "coincidences" in my past and in the present. I have come to realize that the reason I am sitting here is not because I am so smart, but rather because I have been guided all of my life to get to the point where I could write this book. I also know that you, my reader, were also guided to find this book to help you along on your own path of enlightenment.

The Author in Vietnam, 1967.
No one told me my job was to be bait.

22

Miracle in Mexico

As you will recall, during my first past-life regression in June, 1995, my consciousness was taken to the shores of the Dead Sea by the vision of a wooden crucifix. Then, the crucifix disappeared, and I was left suspended above a very dry beach with small, frothy waves lapping on the shore. On the beach were several clay urns, which I instantly knew held the sacred scrolls of the Essenes—the ones they hid in the caves above their community at Qumran. When the therapist asked me if I had known Jesus, I burst out sobbing uncontrollably, unable to respond.

I was left with only the knowledge that I had been there in a past life, and that Jesus was also connected to the Essenes. But I had no idea that there was ever such a connection. It was a mystery that I had to solve. Somehow, my interest in UFOs, and my involvement in UFO research, had led me to an interest in hypnosis, and subsequently to the study of reincarnation.

In October of that year, I was invited to speak at the first International UFO Congress in Mexico City. It was a huge affair, with 36 speakers from all over the world. Among the many speakers was someone with whom I was anxious to speak—retired U.S. Army Command Sergeant Major Robert O. Dean (1929-2018), who was a highly decorated veteran

Robert O. Dean,
U.S. Army Command Sergeant Major (Retired)

of both the Korean and Vietnam Wars. He was one of the more popular and charismatic speakers who often lectured at UFO and New Age conferences in the U.S. and abroad. Born in 1929, Dean was already 63 and retired from the Army for 17 years when we first met two years earlier at a conference in Gulf Breeze, FL. His presentation was stunning, and unlike those of other speakers, many of whom believed the UFO phenomenon began in the 1940s, during World War II. He believed that they have always been here and are at the heart of our major religions. I found myself spellbound by his understanding of the theological implications of the UFO reality.

In retirement, he had let his silver hair grow long, wearing it in a ponytail that matched his silver beard. He looked to me like an Old Testament prophet, and he spoke as one when he began his lecture:

"We are not alone, and we have never been alone," he said as he presented slide after slide of Renaissance and medieval paintings depicting the birth, baptism and crucifixion of Jesus with what seem to be flying saucers and aerial vehicles in the background. One slide showed a painting titled *The Madonna and St. Giovannino* by 15th-Century Italian artist Domenico Ghirlandaio, which hangs in the permanent collection of the Palazzo Vecchio Museum in Florence, Italy.

Many years later, I made the journey to Florence to see this extraordinary painting for myself. It depicts the Madonna holding two infants—one is the baby Jesus, and the other is John the Baptist, but the amazing part is in the background, over her shoulder to the right of the painting. It depicts a scene in which a man and his dog are standing on a high cliff, looking intently upward at a glowing object in the air. The man is shielding his eyes from the glare of the sun with his left hand. A closer look at the object reveals that it is what can only be called a flying saucer, not a comet, star, or planet. If this were the only such painting, it could be dismissed as someone's vivid imagination, but it is not. There

Madonna and St. Giovannino

Courtesy of the Palazzo Vecchio Museum, Florence, Italy.

are many paintings from that era that show disk-shaped objects hovering clearly above a scene from the life of Jesus such as his baptism by John the Baptist, and the moment when the Virgin Mary is told she is to have a son. There are UFOs in the background of a scene in which Jesus is being crucified. In short, the painting of the Madonna with a UFO in the background is not an aberration or a fantasy.

Somehow these paintings reawakened something deep within me and set me on a path to discover the truth about the story of Jesus. After Dean spoke, I approached him and asked him to come to El Paso to speak in March, 1994, at the El Paso Community College, where some of the MUFON meetings were held. That weekend, Bob and I became good friends, and we found that we had much in common, despite our age difference. We had both served in Vietnam, and we had both reached similar conclusions about what was behind the UFO mystery.

But most interesting for me was the fact that we both had a history of miraculous escapes from certain death. Bob also felt that he had guardian angels looking over him. He told me what happened to him after he finished Officer's Candidate School in October, 1950, when he was commissioned as a second lieutenant:

"The next thing I know is I'm on the front lines in Korea, leading an infantry platoon in one of the bloodiest wars we've ever had. Then, the company commander was killed, and I was promoted. Then a series of things began to occur. I seemed to live a charmed life. I was in places I should not have survived. I walked away from helicopter crashes, the only survivor. Men were being killed all around me, and all I got were nicks and a few scratches, and a little shrapnel. It got really eerie. The same thing happened years later in Vietnam, Laos and Cambodia, where I was involved in covert intelligence operations. One time I was sitting in a group with three other guys when a mortar shell dropped right next to us. All of them were killed, but I didn't have a scratch."

I asked him how he went from being a second lieutenant to being a sergeant, and he explained that after Korea, the military downsized and he had a choice of leaving the Army or being reduced in rank. He stayed on as a staff sergeant and eventually worked his way up to the highest non-commissioned officer (NCO) rank—that of command sergeant major. By the time he retired in 1976, he had earned a chest full of medals for bravery under combat and distinguished service.

However, in the early 1960s, while serving as an intelligence analyst at NATO headquarters just outside Paris, he was attached to the Supreme Headquarters Allied Powers Europe (SHAPE) and stumbled upon a highly classified document that changed his life. It was a study initiated in 1961 by British Air Marshall Matthew John Gethin Wiles. It was simply titled, "The Assessment." It covered the mysterious aerial phenomena observed by both allied and enemy pilots during World War II, Korea and beyond that had been seen as a threat of unknown origin. The study, he said, concluded that UFOs were not a military threat, but were of extraterrestrial origin. But the most astonishing conclusion was that they had been monitoring life on Earth for a very, very long time, perhaps thousands of years, and that the human race was a hybrid species, created by extraterrestrials. "This, more than any other thing," he said, "is the reason that our government can never disclose what it knows about UFOs. No politician is willing to be the one who stirs up that nest of controversy."

The U.S. government has denied that any such study ever existed, and many have accused Dean of making it all up. There is no way that Dean can prove that the study existed, because he did not make a copy of it, which would have been highly illegal. Being called a liar has been hard on him, but it didn't stop him from telling his story every chance he had. The document changed his life, causing him to begin a spiritual quest regarding the nature of humanity and the existence of the soul. Dean told me, "The single most important issue here is to understand that each and every one of us is an infinite, spiritual, living, conscious part of God."

Then he told me that he planned to begin working with a hypnotherapist in Arizona, where he lived, to try to unravel the mystery behind the many UFO sightings he had had throughout his life, including his belief that he had been abducted, something he had not revealed to other researchers or to the public. "Oh, I can see why you don't tell many people about that," I said. "Thank you for confiding in me."

"You are one of the few that I would tell," he said, confirming that he and I had a special bond. I couldn't wait to hear the results of his hypnosis sessions, but that would have to wait many months until we met again in Mexico at the International UFO Conference. The morning after our arrival there, I ran into Bob in the hotel restaurant, and we sat together for an early breakfast before the scheduled bus ride to the ancient and mysterious ruins of Teotihuacan, a few miles northeast of Mexico City. I quickly gave him the synopsis of my regression, and, as I spoke, I could see from his expression that he was a bit confused and surprised. In fact, he became teary eyed.

"What's the matter Bob? You seem shaken." I asked.

"I can't believe this!" he said. "This is amazing! Almost the same thing happened to me! I also remembered being there at the time of Jesus. I remembered being one of his followers, and the terrible agony of losing him to the Crucifixion. It took me three hypnosis sessions to get past the emotional block that I had."

"Oh my God!" I said. "I can't believe this!" I wanted to hear more about his experience, but sadly, we were interrupted by two of the other speakers who arrived and wanted to join us. Our conversation would have to wait.

We got separated as we loaded onto the buses for the trip to the pyramids of Teotihuacan, and again afterwards at the luncheon at a nearby restaurant, where in the rush to find a seat, I found myself seated next to a stocky, dark-skinned Mexican man who had been introduced to the group as Dr. Ramirez, who had volunteered to be with the group to attend to any medical issues that might arise. We hardly spoke a word during the meal, but as it was winding down, he turned to me and said in Spanish, "There is something I would like to tell you. I feel that what I have to say is meant for you to hear."

I couldn't imagine what he was talking about, or how he knew I could speak Spanish, but he continued, "I have always been very psychic, and I feel that I am being guided to tell you my story for some reason. Please be patient and hear me out."

"Of course," I said, trying to be polite. "Please go on."

"Several weeks ago, I was watching on TV when a commercial came on advertising an exhibit of artifacts from the Holy Land that were coming to the museum here in Mexico City. One was a box carved out of stone, and it had a lid that had engravings on it. In fact, the whole box was decorated with engravings of some kind."

"What kind of a box was it?" I asked, curious..

"It was used to store the bones of someone. It was a funerary urn in the shape of a box," he said. "The moment I saw it, I recognized it, even though I had never seen it before."

"What do you mean?" I asked, a bit confused.

The Ossuary of the high priest, Caiaphas.

"I knew the box had been used to store the remains of a man named Caiaphas. Do you know who Caiaphas was?

"I don't recall," I answered.

"Caiaphas was the Jewish high priest who condemned Jesus to death," he clarified.

Then, I remembered the Biblical story about how Caiaphas had conspired to have Jesus arrested as a heretic and turned over to the Romans for execution.

By now, Dr. Ramirez had tears streaming down his face, which was contorted in obvious agony. "How did you know it was his box?" I asked.

"Because I knew at that moment that I had been Caiaphas in another lifetime," he answered, now weeping openly. "I went to the museum to see the box, and I found out that I was right. An archaeologist had found it."

The stone box, dated to the First Century AD, I discovered later, was what was called an "ossuary," used only in that period to store the bones of the deceased. This highly decorated box had the name of Caiaphas engraved on its lid, and it is one of the few ancient artifacts testifying to the accuracy of the Biblical story of Jesus.

By now, Dr. Ramirez was choking down tears, but he managed to ask, "I condemned my savior to death! How could I do such a thing? Please help me to understand!"

I was stunned and confused. First Bob Dean told me that he had walked with Jesus, and then a few hours later, this total stranger picked me out of the crowd to ask my help in absolving him of having condemned Jesus to death in a past life. How did he know to pick me? I didn't know what to say or do, but I knew that I had to tell Bob Dean what had happened. Finally, I asked Dr. Ramirez if he would like to go outside to speak more privately, and he agreed.

Then I signaled to Bob to come join us, and all three of us went out to the garden, where I explained to Bob what had happened. I watched Bob's eyes widen in surprise as I relayed the story to him. He could now understand the agony that was clearly apparent in Dr. Ramirez's face. Here was a devout Catholic who had learned that he had condemned his own Lord and Savior to death in a previous life, and who desperately needed answers as to how such a thing could have happened.

I told the doctor about Bob's past-life memories of having been with Jesus and of my own past-life memory as well. He seemed not to be surprised at that, so Bob tried to console him as I translated, "You won't be judged forever for one lifetime; that's why we have many chances to atone for our sins."

"The crucifixion was necessary as a lesson for Mankind," I added. "You were just playing a role, like a play."

But in the end, the best we could do was to tell him we understood and that he was forgiven. We put our arms around him and held him as he sobbed. Bob and I looked at each other in amazement at this strange turn of events. Then the three of us embraced, as a rain shower began to gently wash over us as if, in baptism, we were all forgiven for our sins of long ago.

23

The Reptilians

I came across the reptilians in one of my first abduction cases in 1993 when I formed the local MUFON chapter of in El Paso, TX. Rita Perregrino was a 48-year-old Mexican-American woman who suffered from severe post-traumatic anxiety from a lifetime of abductions, the first of which (as far as she could recall) began as a child where her family lived in a lower-class "barrio" near the international border with Mexico. In our first interview she told me about her experience. She was teary-eyed and shaking visibly as she recalled a scene as if it happened only the day before:

"In 1955, when I was eight years old, a group of us kids were out playing in back of our apartment building. It was summertime, and we got to stay up late. I had the feeling that there was something strange happening, like someone was watching us. Finally, somebody looked up and there was this big, round thing just hanging in the air over a nearby tree. Everybody saw it and nobody knew what it was. It was almost right over us, but we hadn't noticed because it was black and quiet. At first we just ignored it, but then, I remember everyone running to get their parents to come and look. The next thing I remember is that I was in my mother's arms in our apartment, and everyone was very upset because they had been out searching for me for more than two hours. They had even called the police. Then they noticed that I had a wound on my right ankle. It was an oval hole that went clear to the bone, but it wasn't bleeding, and it didn't hurt. I have no idea how I got it, but I know it happened during the time I was missing. At the time, I did not realize that I had been missing, and I didn't know where I had been. My parents didn't take me to the doctor because the wound healed very quickly and there was no infection."

Rita then showed me the scar—a dark, oval indentation just above her right ankle, which looked somewhat like a cigarette burn on her brown skin. As I would soon learn, the scoop mark, often on the leg or ankle, is commonly found on those who have been abducted. A few months later, when she worked up the courage to undergo hypnosis to recall her missing-time experience, she recalled having been playing a game with her friends in which they all held hands in a circle, and was amazed to discover that her feet had left the ground as she was levitated into the awaiting craft. Then, she was in the craft and could see the curved hallway that led to a room where she was placed on a table surrounded by strange-looking creatures.

"They're all over me; they're doing stuff, and I don't know what they're doing."

When asked what the beings looked like, she replied, "I don't want to remember what they looked like.... They were just too ugly, too ugly, too ugly. Their skin is funny.... I don't think I've ever touched a frog, but I think that's what it would feel like."

Later, she would draw a picture of a being that looked like a bi-pedal dinosaur—truly a hideous creature. But she also remembered seeing the Grays, "they take care of things." And then there are the "ones I don't want to look at; they look like bugs, like praying mantises.... They're tall and big and moving around. They all kind of work together."

After the medical procedures were completed, they took Rita to see something that frightened her. "They're showing me things. Oh, no! I don't want to see that! They've

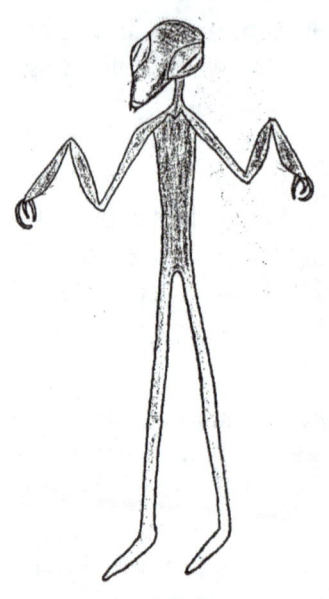

Rita's drawing of a
Mantis being
(from Author's file)

got little things there. They look like little babies, but they're strange looking…. They got them lined up…in long tubes…. They want me to know this is what they are doing, that it's really important to them….They're hooked up to a machine. They're like in glass capsules; there are hundreds. It's kind of like growing plants…. They all look the same. There are the Grey ones and then there are other things, the ones I don't want to look at; they look like bugs, like praying mantises. They say they can make people, or they can make anything they want. They can put things together from different things." (In later hypnosis sessions, Rita was able to recall being shown her own hybrid child in a room full of hybrid children.)

As difficult as it was for her to come face to face with her tormentors, the session had a dramatic healing effect. After her first hypnosis session, which took tremendous courage on her part to endure, she found it to be the beginning of a remarkable transformation. On the Monday following the session, I received an excited phone call from Rita. She said, "I feel as if there is a new sun in the sky just for me! I've never slept so well in my life!" She also found that she was no longer plagued by a strange phobia—she was no longer afraid of babies. Yes, Rita had been terrified of babies and refused to hold one when someone tried to hand one to her at her friend's christening party. She even had trouble handling her own daughter when she was born. After her hypnosis session, Rita realized it was not human babies she feared, but rather it was the babies in the capsules aboard the alien craft that bothered her subconsciously.

My team proceeded to work with Rita at her urging by conducting a series of additional hypnosis sessions in the weeks that followed. What we found was as startling to us as is it was to her. It began with Rita beginning to sob deeply and saying, "I'm home, I'm home. They let me go home."

"Where is home?" I asked.

"It's nothing physical."

"What do you look like?"

"A bright light, kind of when you see lightning.... There's a spark," Rita responded, attempting to describe a place where souls come from and crave to return.

The non-physical beings there explained to her that she had a mission to carry out and that she had to be involved with the "other group" (extraterrestrials) to know what they're doing. When her mission was complete she would be able to go "home" again, something she found very alluring.

After this session, Rita's memories were unblocked, and she was able to remember additional experiences. They showed her a time when she was taken as a child by three reptilians to a world where she was shown something like a zoo, full of strange animals of all sizes and shapes, unlike any she had ever seen before. The purpose was to teach her an important lesson about death. Here, a vicious beast attacked her and killed her. When she left her body, she was met by the Reptilians, also out of their bodies. "If I didn't know better, I would think they're angels.... They changed their physical bodies into transparent bodies.... There seems to be love there. They're up where I am, and they hold me.

Rita's drawing of a reptilian.

(from Author's file)

I tell them I'm angry with them because they didn't protect me..... I want my body back! I'm just a child! I don't know about these things. They're trying to explain to me that nothing really happened. They said, 'Don't worry, we're going to make you 'you' again, and then we're going to take you home.'"

I asked, "How do they get you back together?"

"They say they have duplicate bodies, spares of everybody, and they do this to everybody—that a person isn't just one person, you can be many people and you can be in many places at the same time."

"Go forward now and see what happens next," I suggested.

"It's like a warehouse. They brought it (her duplicate body) for me to look at. They're doing stuff to it. They tell me to look at it and accept it as my own.... They say they do this all the time."

"How do you get into your body?"

"All I had to do was think myself as that body, and it

takes care of itself. Once I get into the body I will still remember what happened and that I would be healthy. I'm afraid my family won't recognize me!"

Finally, after weeping at the loss of her real body, Rita understands the lesson. "It's OK to be in another body if you are the same person. You can die, but you don't die. They are the keepers of knowledge.... They chose their bodies for specific reasons, they never thought of themselves as ugly. They're kind of like lizard-looking—slimy. I don't like looking at them. They tell me not to be angry...."

After the session, Rita was able to see her experience more objectively. "They taught me a lesson on death—that death is not a problem. It may have seemed cold hearted, but I had to understand and accept this process. The body dies but the spirit moves on. Now, I'm not afraid of death anymore."

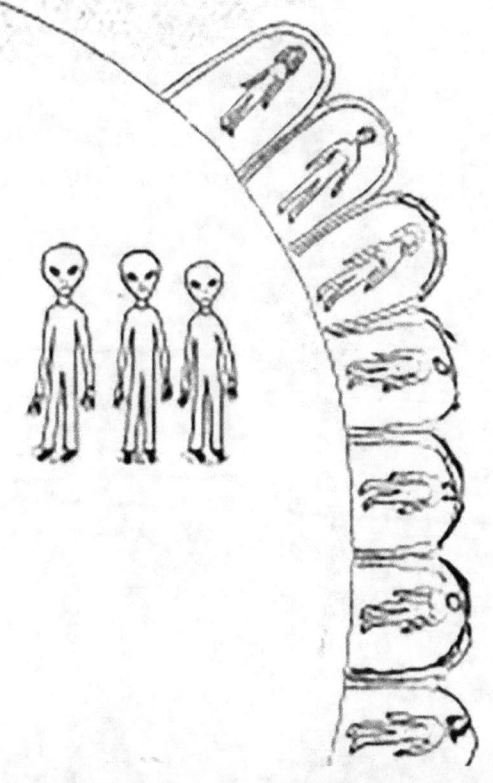

Human bodies in suspended animation.

Drawing by Concepcion Rodriguez

Section IV

Hidden Truths

24

The Reptilian Project

In mid-2003 I received a call at home one evening from my good friend and fellow-abduction researcher, the late Dr. John Mack.

"Joe," he said, "I want you to work with me on a project I'm working on with Barbara Lamb." (Barbara holds a master's degree in behavioral science and is a certified hypnotherapist who began working with UFO experiencers in 1991. She has had numerous cases involving reptilian beings. She actually had a conscious experience with a reptilian in her home. By the time her book, *Alien Experiences*, was published in 2008, she had conducted 1,800 regressions on 560 subjects, making her one of the top abduction researchers in the field.)

"I want to write an article about reptilians," he said, and covering not only our case studies, but also the history of reptilians as described by the ancients. I want to do a thorough and scholarly analysis of the subject. I have an outline worked up, and if you're interested, I'll send it to you."

"Yes, of course! That's a great idea," I replied.

There was no way I would turn down John, no matter what kind of project he suggested. John was one of my heroes. He was one of the most courageous scientists I knew, and he was the most honest. I had traveled with him to Mexico City when he wanted to research cases there. He needed someone he could trust who could also speak Spanish. We interviewed numerous people who had had abduction and close-encounter experiences in and around the nation's capital. He reported on our findings in his second book on the subject, *Passport to the Cosmos* in 1999. He did this in spite of the fact that his earlier book, *Abduction: Human Encounters with Aliens*, had nearly gotten him fired from Harvard. It took a lot of courage for him to risk his brilliant academic credentials to get involved in this controversial subject, and to go public with his findings once again.

However, as brave as he had been about publicly speaking and writing books on the subject of the abduction phenomenon, I knew that he had also been reluctant to say much about the reptilians he came across in his research. He wasn't the only one. When my book, *The God Hypothesis*, (which delves extensively into the subject) was published in 1997, none of the best-known researchers had ever mentioned reptilian beings. I knew they must have been withholding much of their findings for fear of being ridiculed, and if so, they might have also been withholding information on other aspects of the phenomenon they didn't want to accept, like reincarnation, and spiritual growth. Two exceptions were Emmy-award-winning broadcast journalist Linda Moulton Howe and John Carpenter, a trained hypnotherapist and psychiatric social worker who directed MUFON's abduction research. By 1995, he had come across more than a dozen cases in which entities with reptilian features were reported.

I understood why researchers were reluctant to deal with the issue publicly. It was hard enough for the public to accept the Gray aliens, but could they cope with sexually aggressive seven-foot-tall lizard men? Reptilians are too scary, like something out of a B-rated sci-fi movie, too Biblical, and too Satanic-looking. After all, it was a sentient reptile in the Garden of Eden who tempted Eve with the forbidden fruit from the Tree of Knowledge, wasn't it? In my research into the history of sentient reptiles, I was astonished to find many references in the ancient texts to such entities. For example, the Sumerians described a reptilian god named Enki in their ancient clay tablets. According to their story, Enki was the creator of the human race. Additionally, in the Hindu Vedic literature, the reptilians are called the "Nagas," and they are said to live under bodies of water.

In India, one of their oldest books known, called *The Book of Dzyan*, included a story about the serpent race descending from the skies to teach humankind. They are described as beings with human-like faces and tails of dragons. An ancient Indian epic tale, the *Mahabharata*, includes a passage (Section IV, verses 29-33) regarding the Nagas:

"And the gods in cloud-borne chariots came to view the scene so fair....winged suparnas, scaly nagas, deva-rishis pure and high," (Suparnas were winged, bird-like beings.)

The ancient Chinese believed that their first emperors were fathered by celestial dragons, and thus the symbol of the dragon came to denote royalty and, specifically, a divine heritage.

In ancient Egypt, the snake is shown as a powerful being, capable of carrying the soul of the Pharaoh into the afterlife. It was also adopted by them as a symbol of kingship and divine heritage. It can be seen protruding from the center of the forehead of the pharaoh's head dress, home of the mysterious "third eye," in Eastern cultures.

Another example resides in the *Nag Hammadi Texts*, also known as *The Gnostic Gospels*, which tell a different story of Adam and Eve in the Garden of Eden than that found in today's Bible:

"(Eve) looked at the tree, and she saw that it was beautiful and magnificent, and she desired it. She took some of its fruit and ate, and she gave to her husband also, and he ate too. Then their minds were opened. For when they ate, the light of knowledge shone for them.... They knew that they were naked and became enamored of one another. When they saw their makers, they loathed them since they were of beastly forms. They understood very much."

During our long-distance conversations about the project to bring the reptilian beings into the forefront of the UFO phenomena, I asked John if we should include the work of anthropologists Jeremy Narby and Michael Harman. "Yes, of course," he said. "We have to include their findings as well." (I would later discuss their paradigm-shifting work in my 2007 *Rulers of the Earth*.) John and I had, in earlier phone conversations, discussed the amazing work done by these anthropologists, who discovered previously unknown connections to the reptilian beings while studying the shamans of the Amazon rain forest. They were both curious about how the native peoples learned about the uses of thousands of species of plants, which they cultivate for healing, for food, and for communing with otherworldly spirits. The native shamans explained to them on different occasions that they were taught this information by beings from the spirit world; they communed with them by consuming certain hallucinogenic plants found only in the Amazon.

Both Narby and Harman had lived with the Amazonian tribesmen at different times and places to study their practices and belief systems. Both came away from their experiences transformed. Narby, a Stanford-educated Ph.D., wrote about his time with the shamans in his 1998 *The Cosmic Serpent: DNA and the Origins of Knowledge*. The native peoples explained to him that they learned about the uses of plants by ingesting a brew called ayahuasca, which is made from certain plants, which he later learned contained the molecule N,N-Dimethyltryptamine, or DMT for short. This molecule affects the pineal gland, found in the center of the brain, and causes the individual to feel as if he has left ordinary reality and journeyed to other, mysterious dimensions, inhabited by spirit beings. Here, they communicate telepathically with a variety of beings, some ethereal and others whom they perceive to be extraterrestrial. Among the rulers of this strange domain are serpent beings.

When Narby, in the name of research, ingested the brew, he says he found himself "surrounded by two gigantic boa constrictors that seemed 50 feet long. I was terrified."

The snakes began to speak to him telepathically. "They explain to me that I am just a human being. I feel my mind crack, and in the fissures, I see the bottomless arrogance of my presuppositions." He found himself in "...a more powerful reality that I do not understand at all, and that in my ignorance, I did not even suspect existed.... I never felt so completely humble."

As a result, Narby was forced to accept the shaman's belief that spirit beings from other realities guide them and help them survive in the rain forest. He also began to see a correlation between what the shamans have known for thousands of years and what microbiologists are learning today about the DNA molecule. *He concludes that primitive people have learned the secrets of DNA through their out-of-body journeys, and may even have communicated with the consciousness of DNA, which Narby sees as a living, alien intelligence that did not originate on Earth.*

Michael Harner had a similar experience years earlier and wrote about it in his 1980 *The Way of the Shaman*. After ingesting a similar brew, Harner also entered another reality and began receiving telepathic messages from non-human entities who revealed to him the secrets of the origins of life on Earth. The givers of these secrets, he said, "...were giant reptilian creatures, reposing in the depths of my brain." The reptilians projected a vision in which he saw reptilians dropping down from the sky onto a primitive, lifeless Earth in ancient times. They had come to Earth to escape their enemy. "They showed me how they created life on the planet so as to hide within the multitudinous forms and thus disguise their presence.... The dragon-like creatures were thus inside of all forms of life, including man. They are the masters of humanity and the entire planet...."

This seems to me to be an excellent description of the double-helix shape of the DNA molecule, which is like two entwined serpents capable of morphing into every living plant and animal on Earth.

Mack, himself, had a series of paradigm-breaking experiences as he explored non-ordinary states of consciousness with LSD pioneer and psychiatrist, Dr. Stanislav Grof. Grof had 50 years of experience in research into the use of LSD and other meditative states to heal patients with alcoholism and other mental disorders. He is considered one of the principal developers of what is known as "transpersonal psychology," which seeks to integrate the spiritual and transcendent aspects of the human experience.

Mack had been raised in a secular family with no religious dogma to blur his inquisitive nature. He had to learn about other states of reality—other dimensions—by experiencing them for himself. But even his previous work with Grof did not prepare him for a major challenge to his beliefs when he realized that the abductees he was studying were not crazy, but were, in fact, experiencing another reality—one just as real as the one he was accustomed to. In *Passport to the Cosmos*, he says:

"My own view of a secular universe, devoid of consciousness and intelligence beyond the brain, gave way little by little over several decades and now seems quite absurd. But it happened because I had what was, for me, incontrovertible experiential evidence of transcendent reality... (which was) contrary to my world view and for which I have been unable to find a conventional, material, or psychological explanation."

Over the many years of our association, Mack and I had numerous discussions about the ability of these beings we call "aliens" to move in and out freely from the reality (dimension) we are familiar with to other realities or dimensions. We were particularly taken by the reports we were getting from our subjects that they were taken into another dimension by the beings. We both had almost identical cases in which a reptilian being seemed to zip open a portal from its dimension, in the middle of a bedroom, and take a woman with him through the portal into a cavern-like place that was definitely not a ship, but a seemingly underground location. In both cases, the reptilian had sex with the woman and then returned her to her room through the same portal.

Mack was concerned with the idea of two different realities. He asked me, "Joe, if she was raped in a different reality, did it really happen?"

A witness's drawing of a reptilian being. (from Author's file)

"Well," I replied, "it seems to me that if it was real for her, and her bruises and needle marks are real, then we have to accept that it really did happen. If we don't, we aren't honoring her report of the traumatic event she experienced. The trauma is real, so I think we have to accept her report of the event as real. Also, these cases aren't that unusual. We have many cases in which the subjects state that they were taken out of their bodies into another dimension where medical procedures were performed on them. If we're not going to accept these events as real, then where does that leave us? Are we only going to report on activities in our dimension and consider the rest as mere fantasy?"

"Yes, of course," he agreed. "You're right. We are obligated to divulge everything we discover. It would be dishonest to exclude information simply because it was too weird or hard to believe. I think we both have crossed that line already. There is a reality behind the abduction experience, we both agree on that, but the question is whose reality is it?"

These discussions between the two of us and Barbara Lamb went on for several months via telephone calls and email. Finally, Mack grew frustrated with the difficulty of coordinating the work of three researchers by long distance. In late August 2004 he suggested we get the ball rolling by presenting our material at the International UFO Conference in Laughlin, NV, to be held in March 2005. Both Barbara and I agreed to get our presentations together by then.

But then Mack added, "I have to go to London next month to speak at a conference, so I'll call you when I get back." He explained that he was to speak at a conference on Lawrence of Arabia, the topic of a book he authored in 1977 which won him the Pulitzer Prize. Sadly, those were the last words we ever heard from him.

He never returned from London. After his presentation that evening, September 27, 2004, while walking back to his hotel, John stepped off a curb and was run over.

The following day I received a call from one of his close friends giving me the shocking news. I didn't want to believe it. As the most-respected spokesman in the UFO/abduction research field, he was needed by very many people. How could we carry on without him? There was no one like him to take his place. There was no one with his credentials and his brilliance capable of speaking as eloquently and with such authority on the subject. Then it dawned on me that his tragic death also meant that he would not have his chance to serve as a witness to the reality of the reptilian presence in the abduction experience.

Mack's portion of the presentation was never completed, and his unique perspective on this amazing topic was lost forever. Barbara and I went ahead with our contributions in Laughlin, but John's unique insights and his case studies were never revealed. All of his material and files were left in his estate, which was controlled by his heirs, who were not interested in the subject. All we had left were a few pages of hastily written notes that he had used to create the outline we had received at the beginning of the project.

One last postscript that he would have wanted me to mention is that neither of us had uncovered any evidence that any world leaders are, in fact, shape-shifting reptilians, as some have claimed. There is no need for wild speculation and hyperbole when the facts themselves are so incredible.

25

The Hunchbacked Woman

There have been many efforts throughout the years attempting to prove that reincarnation is real. Books such as *Children's Past Lives* by Carol Bowman and *Life After Life* by Raymond Moody are excellent examples. But perhaps the best known is the work of Dr. Ian Stevenson (1918-2007), a Canadian-born American psychiatrist who founded the Division of Perceptual Studies at the University of Virginia, dedicated to the study of the paranormal.

Stevenson also helped to found The Society for Scientific Exploration in 1982 to investigate cases of possible reincarnation and near-death experiences. He wrote 14 books documenting such cases from around the world, but his most popular book for the general public was his 1997 work, *Where Reincarnation and Biology Intersect*. He discovered that people who remembered past lives could recall not only the details of that life, but they also relived the emotions felt by the person in the previous life, and often displayed scars, birthmarks and deformities relating to injuries or traumas incurred in that life. They often had irrational phobias, illnesses and unusual talents brought forth from previous lifetimes.

During his 40 years of fieldwork, which took him all over the world, he reported on 3,000 cases of children who vividly remembered past lives. In one case, typical of the many he investigated, Stevenson recounted the story of a newborn girl in Sri Lanka who screamed whenever she was carried near a bus or a bath. Later, when she was old enough to talk, he said, she remembered a previous lifetime as a girl of 8 or 9 who drowned after a bus knocked her into a flooded rice paddy. Later investigation found the family of just such a girl whose family lived only a few kilometers away, and were able to verify the facts of the girl's story.

Stevenson found that between the ages of two and four, many children spontaneously begin speaking about details of previous lives. This phenomenon continues until about five or six, but by eight, the children generally stop speaking about past lives. The memories are more vivid and last longer if the child had a violent death in the previous life. Stevenson's contribution to the field did not include hypnotic regression; he relied on the children's conscious memories and investigations meant to verify their claims.

Although Dr. Stevenson's methodology has great merit in helping to convince critics that reincarnation is real, there are those, like myself and many others, who do not need convincing. Those of us who have undergone regressive hypnosis know that our recovered memories reflect real past lives, and therefore we do not need the use of the scientific method to help us believe in reincarnation. In all my years as a past-life regression therapist, I never once thought about trying to prove that a past life remembered by one of my subjects was real.

The whole point of the regression was to help people understand that they are spiritual beings who have lived before and will live again after death. The purpose of hypnotherapy is to heal, to resolve troubling issues, and to help people to find their purpose in their present life. It is not to prove anything about the reality of reincarnation. Even if a person walks away from a hypnosis session as a skeptic, unwilling to accept that their past-life memories were real, as long as their phobia is relieved, or their fear of death has dissipated, it just doesn't matter if the past life was real. In fact, the healing of phobias and discovering purpose in life are proof enough. Psychiatrists know that healing occurs only after the root cause has been discovered.

But for those who need evidence and hard facts to accept the reality of past lives, one only needs to hear the story of someone who actually proved that his past life was real. I ran into someone who had done just that at a UFO conference in 1999. That is one of the best things about UFO conferences—you never know whom you are going to run into. They attract the most interesting and amazing persons, and the conference creates an atmosphere in which people are willing to share their bizarre experiences with everyone, whereas back home they have never shared their stories with anyone for fear of being ridiculed.

Such is the case of Captain Robert L. Snow, commander of the homicide branch of the Indianapolis Police Department for 38 years, and retired in 2007. Snow could be described as a hard-nosed detective who used his powers of deduction and attention to detail in tracking down murderers and having them imprisoned. He was not one to believe in New Age "bunk" or stories of the paranormal. There could be no more skeptical person when it came to such things as reincarnation or out-of-body experiences, so when he met a psychologist at a party, he was less than intrigued when she told him she used hypnosis to help people remember their past lives. He told her, rather insultingly, "I think past-life regression is probably just people with a lot of imagination. Probably just people who want to blame their problems on something they can't be held accountable for now. Besides, if it was true, then how come no one's ever proved they've lived a past life?"

After his little speech, the psychologist politely challenged him to test his beliefs. "She basically dared me to find out for myself if it was as phony as I thought it was." Rather than being branded a "chicken," and having been badgered for several months about his failure to make an appointment to be hypnotized, he finally agreed to take the dare, even though he didn't believe in hypnosis and believed that it would be a waste of time. Nevertheless, when the time came, he admits he was scared.

In his 1999 *Looking for Carroll Beckwith*, Snow relates how he finally relented and found himself sitting in an over-stuffed chair in the office of Dr. Mariellen Griffith, a psychologist who specialized in hypnotic regressions. But he was still doubtful that he could be hypnotized. "I felt sure that I was much too strong-willed to be hypnotized and that I would instead spend a very uncomfortable hour with a person who would try to convince me that I was hypnotized, when I knew I wasn't." But during the session, "something happened, something so bizarre and startling I would have screamed in surprise if I hadn't already lost my breath."

He had been regressed to a past life at a time when he was a caveman, living in an Alpine valley. "I stood in a valley. I don't mean that I just imagined or daydreamed that I stood in a valley, or that I just saw a valley in my mind. I was there. I could see the trees and thick underbrush all around me. I could hear the chirping of birds in the nearby branches, and I could feel the tingling breeze of a slight wind blowing in my face.... It seemed as if I had suddenly walked through a door into another world."

Afterward, he rationalized that it was "simply my mind dredging up old memories, or perhaps bits of movies and books, from my subconscious and recasting them into a story line." Even so, he later said, it was so realistic that "it was like discovering the most fascinating ride imaginable at an amusement park, and I wanted more of it. It had become the most fascinating experience of my life...."

After leading him through a life of hardship at a time when there were few people on Earth, and when he lived alone in a cave, she took him to the last day of his life and asked him what he had learned. "That it's not good to be alone, that you need someone," he said.

Then the therapist led him to a more recent lifetime and a scene began to appear, a scene as clear and real as the previous life. He found himself on a city street in the late 19th Century, complete with horses pulling carriages and gas streetlamps along the sidewalk. He was wearing a fancy shirt and jacket, and he was carrying a fancy cane, "more of a status symbol than a crutch." He was walking down a street to meet a very beautiful woman named Amanda—his wife. After eating at a sidewalk café and ordering wine, he recalled that his name was Jack. Then, he recalled that he was an artist and visualized a large room full of paintings with skylights and lots of windows—his studio. He could see canvasses with landscapes and many portraits. However, he recalled the paintings weren't selling and he was always short of money. He hated painting portraits, but they paid better than his landscapes, which were, at best, mediocre.

During the session he remembered that his mother had died of a blood clot, which elicited strong emotions. Then he recalled one particular painting that stood out from the rest. It was an unforgettable portrait of a hunchbacked woman. It reminded him of the fact that as much as he hated painting portraits, they were his main source of income.

Then, the therapist took him to the last day of that life, which he recalled as being 1917, and asked him what lessons he learned from that life. The answer: "We should have had children. We were happy, but we didn't have any children. I don't think Amanda could have children."

After the session, he was embarrassed, and he berated himself for not acting like a captain of detectives, but more "like some kind of nut. I realized that my earlier belief that I couldn't be hypnotized had obviously been wrong.... I had lost at least partial control of my ability to think before I spoke.... I knew that for the past hour I had acted like one of those kooks and weirdos I'd always rolled my eyes at."

So, he decided to set out to do what he did best—investigate the mystery and prove to himself and to the therapist that an American painter who lived for a while in Paris never existed. He was certain he would find nothing that verified the reality of that past-life memory. Fortunately for him, he had recorded the entire hypnosis session, which provided him with 28 statements of fact that he could disprove.

But even as he began his investigation, and having convinced himself that there was a logical explanation for what he had seen, he remained perplexed. "I still couldn't shake the feeling that I had just experienced something tremendously profound and important. I still couldn't get over the vividness or the feeling of reality." One of the reasons he did not want to believe that he had actually lived a past life was his religious upbringing in a Christian home. Reincarnation played no role in his understanding of his faith; it had never been mentioned in any sermon, and, he believed, it was not in the Bible.

His first investigative step was to go to libraries and bookstores seeking the painting of the hunchbacked woman he had seen so clearly while hypnotized. He spent months and many hundreds of hours searching art books and questioning gallery owners looking for the painting, to no avail. He felt if he found the painting in a book, it would explain how he might have seen it before, but just forgot about it. The search would have been much easier if he knew the artist's name, but he only remembered that he said his name was "Jack." It became glaringly apparent that whoever the painter was, he wasn't famous enough to find easily.

A year went by, and he had given up the search; he decided to just go on with his life. But the image of the painting was still vivid in his mind. So, he and his wife decided to take a vacation to New Orleans, to relax, visit the famous French Quarter, and to browse through the many antique stores for which the city is famous. The trip was well earned. As a homicide detective for so many years, he had witnessed far too many shocking scenes that were hard to forget. But nothing prepared him for what was about to happen. On the last day of the vacation, while looking through many of the antique stores on Royal Street, they found many art galleries and decided to enter a few just for fun. Upon entering a small gallery, his wife decided to go upstairs to look at the modern art, while he browsed on the first floor. At the end of a row of paintings, an easel stood holding a portrait. He glanced at it and was about to go past when he stopped abruptly, "as if running into a glass wall." Whirling around, he stared open-mouthed at the portrait, and experienced a shock like none he had experienced before. It was the portrait of the hunchbacked woman.

"I wasn't prepared to find it like this, ...to just stumble onto it by chance in an obscure little shop a thousand miles from home. It was just too much of a coincidence, I told myself. Far too much of a coincidence.... As I stood motionless with my eyes closed, still in shock, in front of the portrait, electricity seeming to crackle off my skin, I could once again see the hunchbacked woman, whose portrait I now stood

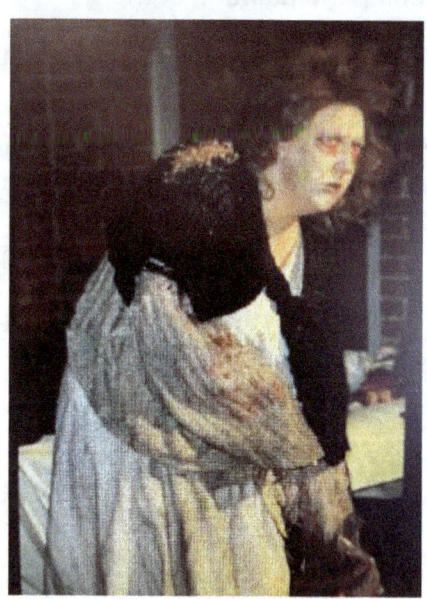

The Hunchbacked Woman
(from Author's file)

in front of. I could see her posing erectly in the studio, with stiff, raised shoulders. While it defied logical explanation, I was never more sure of anything in my life. This was the portrait I had seen myself painting." Then, the attendant gave him a brochure with a biographical sketch of the artist—everything he needed to reopen the cold case.

The affirmation that he had lived a past life hit him like a thunderbolt. From then on, the mystery unfolded quickly. He found the name of the painter—J. Carroll Beckwith, a somewhat obscure artist who died in 1917, just as he had remembered. Knowing that, he returned to the libraries and museums and found a great deal about the man, including his 17,000-page diary. He had to read every page, but he was able to verify nearly all of the 28 facts that were recorded on that audio tape of his regression. The one difference was that Beckwith's first name was James, not "Jack," as Snow had recalled. Then he found out that "Jack" is often a nickname used by men named James. In any case, it was undeniable. Instead of proving that the therapist was wrong and that reincarnation does not happen, he found just the opposite: "There was no other explanation. With the level of proof I had, if this had been a criminal case, I would have been absolutely certain of a conviction."

Ultimately, homicide detective Robert L. Snow visited Beckwith's grave in New York and realized that he had to accept the truth. The world he once assumed was real was not the true reality. He had to reevaluate everything he ever believed in, including the religion he was born into, which he had accepted without question—one that did not teach about, or ever mention, reincarnation. That was a hard pill to swallow for someone who once scoffed at those "kooks" who believed in reincarnation. One could say that it is like the old joke: his karma ran over his dogma on that day.

26

Soul Transfers

By mid-1994 the El Paso chapter of MUFON was going strong. Our monthly meetings were announced in the newspaper, making it clear that the public was welcome for a fee of $5. We had a wide variety of people wandering in off the street to sit in on the meetings, which were held in the downtown public library. On April 30 I noticed an old, Mexican man who came shuffling in to sit quietly at the back of the room. For some reason, I was curious about why he had come here.

Attendance in those days was between 35 and 70 people; each one would be required to sign in and include their phone number and address so we could send them a notice regarding the time and place of the next meeting, as well as the names of guest speakers we occasionally brought in from out of town. The money we collected was used to pay the expenses for guest speakers, such as Whitley Strieber, Dr. John Mack, Bob Dean, Lynn Buchanan (a remote viewer trained in the secret CIA program in the 1970s) and many more. The agenda at each meeting, when there was no guest speaker, was to have a member of the group stand and give a testimony about their UFO/abduction experiences, and then we left time for questions or comments. Often, others would stand and give their own testimony. These meetings were also where we recruited UFO experiencers to be part of our research program into the abduction phenomenon.

After the meeting, I approached the old man at the back of the room and engaged him in conversation. For some reason I felt that he might want to share his own experience with me. He seemed pleased to get some attention, and he introduced himself as Concepción Rodriquez, a retired salesman who was a lifelong resident of El Paso. He began by explaining that he suffered from very poor sight and, therefore, he was forced to stop working recently at age 50, although he looked considerably older. Then he began telling me about some very strange experiences he had in the years when his sales job required him to regularly drive the remote roads of southern NM to towns such as Hobbs, Roswell, Carlsbad and Tucumcari, often late at night in the summer months to avoid the heat of the day.

I decided to sit with him, take out my notebook, and conduct an interview on the spot. He said that when he was about 30, in mid-1974, he had a frightening experience driving between Carlsbad and Hobbs late at night. The first thing he noticed was a bright light traveling fast across the desert towards his car. He thought it was a plane on fire about to crash, but then it just vanished. A few moments later, it was behind him, so he reasoned it must be a cop car chasing after him. That thought left him when the light stopped and hovered just above his car. "It was the size of an aircraft carrier," he told me.

"Then the gauges in my car just went haywire, and a green light filled my car. The next thing I remember is waking up on the side of the road. My radio came back on, and the announcer said it was 3:45 am. That's when I realized that I had lost 3½ hours. I had been about 15 minutes from Hobbs when I saw the light, so I should have arrived around 12:15. I was shaking and so scared that I thought I had to tell someone. I drove to the Hobbs police station and sat outside in my car thinking about what I would tell them. But then I realized there was nothing they could do, and they would just think I was drunk or crazy. So, I just went home and went to bed."

One would think that his story would have been shocking to me, but the fact was I already had several people tell me almost identical stories. It seemed to me at the time that those lonely New Mexico roads were not a good place to be late at night. We had already interviewed three others who experienced missing time on those same deserted highways late at night. In one case, a family of four was driving at night across southern New Mexico from El Paso to Yuma, AZ, when a very bright light appeared over their car, which suddenly lost power and coasted to the side of the road. Even though they all experienced a period of three hours of missing time, they were not willing to undergo hypnosis, so we can't be sure what transpired. However, the psychiatric manual used by psychologists says nothing about shared amnesia. It's just not supposed to happen, unless they were all drunk or on drugs, which they were not.

Based on the brief interview with Mr. Rodriguez, I invited him to meet with the rest of my team, particularly our psychiatrist, with the objective being to consider him for a hypnosis session to recover what happened during those 3½ hours of missing time. After being evaluated by our team psychiatrist, we determined to go through with the hypnosis session, which he was eager to try because he was desperate to learn what had happened to him that night, 20 years ago. We scheduled the session for the following week, and he fell into a deep trance quite easily as our team hypnotherapist guided him gently towards that fateful night. He recalled being in his car when the greenish light filled the interior, and he felt immobilized. "They're pulling the car up in that light, and the car goes up through a hole in the bottom of the giant craft."

He soon found himself lying on an operating table surrounded by four gray beings with large heads and big black eyes. "They have needles in their hands and they're doing procedures on me. There's also some human-looking ones in the background." During the medical procedures, they use a rectal probe to take semen samples, then they take liver samples and use the needles to probe his nose, ears and the back of his skull. But perhaps the most interesting thing that he witnessed on board the ship was a wall lined with glass-like containers, each one holding the naked body of a human, as if in suspended animation. "They didn't tell me why they had those bodies, but it seemed to me they could be woken up at any time."

The idea that the aliens kept humans in containers in suspended animation was new to our team at the time, because we still had not known about Rita Perregrino's experience being given a duplicate body after the reptilian beings she was with allowed her to be mauled to death by an otherworldly beast.

She said at that time the beings have duplicate bodies of everyone. But then in 1993, when investigative journalist Linda Moulton Howe published *Glimpses of Other Realities Vol. II,* I was surprised to discover that she had found another abductee who spoke extensively about the fact that the beings regularly transfer souls into cloned bodies for various reasons.

The case concerned Linda Porter from Porterville, CA, who recalled a scene under hypnosis when she was taken aboard a craft. She said, "I was shown...a room with very tall, clear tube-like containers or cylinders on a raised platform which seemed to be at the center of the room. Inside these tubes—standing upright, naked, and appearing to be asleep—were humans, or at least they looked human to me. They looked like they were in suspended animation."

In a later session she recalled being on a craft with a praying-mantis being and being shown a man who was very close to death, lying in a rectangular container. She watched as "...his soul was then lifted up out of his dying body. It left the body in the area of his solar plexus.... The soul floated across the room to another body that looked like the man would have appeared at about 25.... The soul floated above the new body, which was standing upright, outside the tube.... It then descended, entering the body at the top of the back of the head (and descending) all the way down to the area midway between the shoulder blades. It then merged into the body totally and settled in front of the spinal column in the area of the solar plexus.... The body at this point took on an "occupied" look, as if the person were merely asleep." It was explained to her that the reason they take tissue samples from abductees when they are quite young is to have the tissue in reserve "in case a new body becomes necessary later on."

When she became gravely ill at 17, she was put on a table by the beings and rendered unconscious. "My soul was then lifted up and out of my body and placed into another one that looked exactly like it!" (Pp. 256-262).

Dr. Karla Turner, in her 1994 *Masquerade of Angels,* reported another case of duplicate bodies, in which she documents the case of Ted Rice, who remembered an experience with reptilians very similar to that of Rita's. In early childhood, Ted, who was raised in Alabama, developed psychic abilities and grew up believing he had "spirit guides." But as an adult, his experiences began to parallel those of UFO abductees, including night visitations by a strange being he called Volmo, who walked right through his bedroom wall and spirited him away. Volmo would instruct him in spiritual truths, but he was a very unusual spirit guide.

Ted eventually realized that Volmo wasn't human-looking, but rather was "God-awful ugly!.... I reckon he's 6-1/2 feet tall and massive. His eyes don't look human; they're dark, sort of yellow-gold, but his mouth is the worst part, it looks like a big fish mouth with sharp teeth. There are four webbed fingers on his hands.... They look claw-like because he's got these long, pointed nails on each finger." Although Ted had never heard of reptilians, it is clear that his "spirit guide," Volmo presented as a reptilian.

Under hypnosis, Ted was able to recall a strange experience that occurred when he was about 8. He was placed by the reptilians on an operating table and was forced to drink a green liquid that made him violently ill. In a short time, he was floating above his body, watching it lying motionless. Then a strange thing happened. "Something cloudy and formless began to rise up from the small body.... 'It's my soul,'" he thought in amazement.

One of the beings then attached wires to the body and to a rectangular black box, and Ted's soul was slowly sucked into the box. Next, the being used a laser-like instrument to decapitate his body, allowing the blood to drain into a vat. Another being went to a locker and removed a body identical to Ted's, completely naked. They moved the duplicate body over to a tilted table and set it down; then they took the black box and set it on his chest.

Ted could see the naked body suddenly begin to jerk in short spasms. Then the chest started to rise and fall, as if the body were now breathing. Soon, Ted found himself in his new body. Then a tall blonde, human-looking being arrived

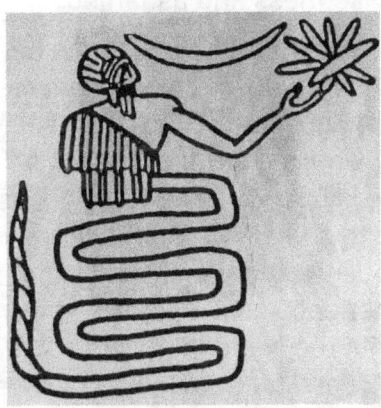

Enki, the Sumerian Serpent God, creator of the human race, is seen here in an illustration from a Mesopotamian cylindrical seal, giving warning to man of the imminent flood.

(Courtesy of Zechariah Sitchin, *When Time Began.*)

and explained to him that the procedure was necessary for Ted to fulfill his purpose in life. He was made to understand that he was part of "an experiment for the continuity of life, in some way involved with the final stages of life on Earth."

There are important lessons to be taken from these cases, which are totally unrelated, yet startlingly similar. We can infer that these superior beings have long practiced the science of soul transfers from humans to duplicate bodies for various purposes, mostly mysterious. But in some cases, the purpose is to heal a dying body or to enhance the individual's psychic abilities. Who knows what other objectives they might have? But whatever they are, they have been doing this for a very long time, even as far back as the creation of the human race. One ancient Jewish text, known as the Haggadah, includes this interesting description of Adam and Eve after they ate the forbidden fruit:

"The first result was that Adam and Eve became naked. Before, their bodies had been overlaid with a horny skin, and enveloped with the cloud of glory. No sooner had they violated the command given them than the cloud of glory and the horny skin dropped from them, and they stood there in their nakedness and ashamed."

Could the first prototype humans have appeared to be part reptilian? If reptilian beings were responsible for our genetic engineering, such a conclusion seems reasonable. One researcher who is convinced this is the true history of the human race is R.A. Boulay, whose books, *Flying Serpents and Dragons*, and *Dragon Power*, trace the hidden history of our species. Boulay's keen analytical mind, honed through 30 years of experience as a cryptologist for the U.S. government, mostly with the National Security Agency, helped him to build a strong case for human reptilian heritage.

Referring to the reptilian gods of the Sumerian stories, Boulay says that by combining the characteristics of the native ape man with their own saurian nature, the beings produced the first humans, who were half human and half reptile. In a war between the saurian creator gods and the human-looking ones, Boulay says that these first prototypes were ultimately destroyed, resulting in *Homo Sapiens Sapiens*, or wise apes, as we call them.

A recurring theme in ancient texts is the battle between human-looking gods and reptilian gods. Here, the Greek snake-god, Typhon, battles with Zeus.
Note the double-helix-like arrangement of the serpent's tail.

(Courtesy Z. Sitchin, *The War of Gods and Men*.)

Chapter 27

Scientific and Religious Beliefs

Deniers of my thesis will argue that I haven't provided any hard evidence to support my audacious claims. Much of my argument is based on information provided by people who have been hypnotized. Certainly, they argue, hypnosis is not a reliable method of discovering truth. It wouldn't even be accepted in a court of law! Furthermore, hypnosis isn't reliable because it is thought to evoke false memories – figments of the imagination.

But, in defense, let me say that in more than 30 years of experience as a certified hypnotherapist, I have tested my subjects who were in a hypnotic trance to accept false premises that I purposely inserted into the hypnosis session, and never once did any subject accept them. I believe strongly that hypnosis evokes real memories when it is administered by a qualified therapist.

As for references to ancient documents, thousands of years old, they record parables written anonymously by unknown persons. No such documents would be admissible in a modern court of law. The outlandish references to reptilian beings who transfer souls from people into cloned bodies are so absurd that few people are likely to risk believing them! To refer to such stories as "myths" suggest that we know that they are fictional, but we do not know that.

Quoting from ancient sources is no different from what priests and ministers do every day, even though most are either totally ignorant of the true history of the texts they cite, or purposely preach false doctrine. Furthermore, I cite a great many sources—all banned by the Church—that support my position and past-life memories. I seriously doubt that many clerics have ever even read those documents, or that they are even aware that they exist.

Let's remind ourselves of how difficult it was to create a scroll and write something down. It required intense labor to create paper, and/or prepare a skin to scroll quality. And there were very few people with writing skills. For a subject to be written down, it had to be important.

Interestingly, when you combine the information from ancient documents and compare it with the information conveyed by modern experiencers under hypnosis, there is a correlation. Is this correspondence just coincidental? What about the mythical stories of dragons? Why would people from all over the world who rarely if ever communicated with each other have similar images of dragons, mythical or other dimensional?

I admit that these criticisms have some validity. I am asking much of you to accept the bizarre truth about the universe we live in.

And finally, the skeptic will argue, that I have made no effort herein to utilize the scientific method upon which modern civilization is built. Therefore, this book cannot be in any way objective. It must be totally subjective and thus unreliable.

The scientific method was developed as a way to focus on what is measurable because measurement is how we define reality. The scientific method assumes that what you see is what you get, but the whole scientific paradigm was shattered when it became clear through quantum physics that physical reality is an illusion that requires being observed.

The massive technical progress achieved in the Western World is directly traceable to the scientific method, so it is difficult to dismiss it. Where would we be if we threw away everything that science has brought us? We would have no electric lights, cars, TV, radio, air conditioning, *etc.,* but neither would we have nuclear weapons nor would we live in the shadow of the existential threat of our planet being incinerated by climate change. Only time will tell if what the scientific method brought us was all "progress."

We routinely experience the cognitive dissonance that comes with attempts to use the scientific method in a practical way in our everyday world. Science concludes, for example, that consuming dairy products can increase our cholesterol, which can lead to arteriosclerosis, which can kill us with heart attacks, so many of us exclude dairy products from our diets. Then other researchers, using the same scientific method, conclude that eggs and cheese are our only natural source of Vitamin K2, which keeps calcium out of soft tissues like arteries, which prevents arterial calcification and guides calcium into bones and teeth instead. So dairy or no dairy? It drives us all to distraction. Why? Science has become too narrowly focused and has lost sight of the wholeness of life itself, including our bodies.

I am reminded of when I was invited by billionaire Bob Bigelow to go to Las Vegas and meet with his investigative team at the National Institute for Discovery Science (NIDS), just as my book, *The God Hypothesis*, was being published. He liked it so much that he bought many copies and handed them out to the scientists on his team. I spent a day meeting with him and his team as they described the research they were conducting at the Skinwalker Ranch in northeastern Utah. They explained to me that the objective of the study was to use the scientific method to study the paranormal activity that occurred with great frequency there.

His intention, after collecting the data, was to publish articles in mainstream scientific journals to get more scientists interested in such things as UFOs or UAPs (Unidentified

Arial Phenomena), cattle mutilations, and other events of high strangeness. After hearing what they had to say, I told them I didn't think it would work, because using three-dimensional technology to study possibly fifth-dimensional phenomena isn't feasible. I suggested that they conduct a parallel study using scientific remote viewers to uncover the source of the phenomena they were experiencing.

My idea didn't go over well, because remote viewing, which involves specialists who have been trained to use their psychic abilities to "view" phenomena at a distance, was not considered to be scientific, even though it had been used successfully for years by covert government agencies to spy on our nation's enemies. Ultimately, Bigelow shut down the project after ten years of study and experimentation without much success in publishing scientific papers.

The team did, however, learn a great deal that could not be published – almost all of his team members, as well as Bigelow himself, had paranormal experiences at the ranch, some of them quite frightening. Even scarier, many people who spend time at the ranch, even to this day, carry paranormal experiences back home with them, where even their family members are affected.

In a 2024 You Tube video, Bigelow courageously admitted that as a child he had been visited by small, non-human entities in his bedroom at night – a sure sign that he is an abductee, an admission that would certainly explain his life-long interest in UFO phenomena. However, making such an admission could undermine his credibility among anyone who did not have such experiences.

Using scientific methods on Skinwalker Ranch back in the '90s and more recently on the popular TV show of the same name, revealed anomalies, but it didn't solve anything, because what occurs on the ranch is unexplainable with our current knowledge.

I am certain that deep in the bowels of our darkest and most secretive agencies of the U.S. government there are those who have known for many years what I have revealed in this book. There are even some very high-ranking politicians and officials who have been briefed about the real truth about the UFOs, (UAPs) mystery. But they are not about to tell the public what they know, for fear of the reaction from the world's powerful religious institutions and their devotees. There is absolutely no upside for the government, or any politician, to ever reveal the truth.

Most priests and ministers stick with the accepted Christian program, as they have long depended upon support from their faithful adherents. Similarly, most scientists are forced to stay within their scientific-method paradigm — to be accepted and keep the grant money flowing to their coffers. The establishment, whether secular or religious, protects its own and scoffs at those who see it differently. Many people, myself included, receive great solace from religion. Many people love their scientific jobs, and science shields them from attack by making it almost impossible to criticize professionals without having advanced academic degrees better than the person being attacked. Nonetheless, there are consequences for any professional who moves outside the accepted norms. Scientists are not Inquisitors, but recall the scathing attacks on John Mack for concluding that experiencers are not insane and that "alien" abduction accounts can be valid areas of professional research. Dr. John Mack was a brave man for stepping outside of his paradigm, and he remains widely respected.

But the truth is that Science knows that the universe is not at all like the one they have cherished for so long. Certainly by now most are aware of the work in quantum physics that has totally destroyed the notion of objective reality and the concept of the scientific method. Quantum physics — the study of subatomic particles, like electrons, photons, protons, and many more has defied scientists' ability to use the scientific method to measure them.

For example, when attempting to study photons, they discovered that photons are not distinct particles, but rather they are more like energy waves with no physical component. The weirdest discovery was that quantum particles are only material when they are being observed by the scientists. Otherwise, they change into energy waves. The conclusion that stunned the scientific community was that the entire material world may only be material because it is being observed. But by whom?

Perhaps it is the job of the ancient creator gods, the Watchers, to keep the illusion of materiality in place. In any case, one thing is clear—the photons responded to the behavior of the scientists. The observer and the observed are somehow connected. The scientists affect the outcome of the experiment with their minds!

As scientists tried to comprehend the odd behavior of these basic building blocks of the physical world, they continued to be taken aback by their other mysterious properties. Under certain conditions, subatomic particles appear to communicate with each other over vast distances, instantaneously, like twins who feel each other's pain.

At first, the researchers did not want to accept this result because such behavior would violate Einstein's theory of relativity that states that nothing can travel faster than the speed of light. Einstein's protégé David Bohm ultimately realized that the information wasn't traveling through time and space from one location to another, but rather existed in another dimension that superseded time and space.

Furthermore, because everything in the physical universe is made up of subatomic particles, Bohm concluded that everything in the universe must be interconnected at the quantum level, and thus, the notion of objectivity is unsound. We cannot objectively study something of which we are a part.

He concluded that all points in space and time are the same. Nothing is truly separated from anything else. Bohm detailed his findings in his 1951 *Quantum Theory*, where he stated that the classical concepts of physics are no longer relevant because they rely on the idea that the world can be broken into distinct elements that can be described with high precision because they are separate from one another. However, he states that the findings of quantum physics "clearly imply the indivisible unity of all interacting systems."

Bohm shocked the world of science by pointing out that the universe is characterized by oneness, rather than separateness. Any effort to study the world around us, therefore is subjective, because we are all part of that world and intrinsically connected to everything in it. We are truly all one, whether it seems that way or not. Now we just need to adopt that conclusion and its implications and build a new world of understanding.

You may say that the Catholics were more successful in keeping their desired religious perspectives intact and suppressed than they were in suppressing scientific knowledge, as even when Galileo was under house arrest for saying the planets revolve around the sun, he continued writing, and ultimately science won. However, within Christianity, reincarnation and any reference to us going around the Earth reincarnation wheel is still not openly discussed.

The same can be said of most of the literature in science, being based as it is upon the false assumption that things are separable when they are not. We are at a point perhaps not unlike the days following the burning in 48 BC of the ancient world's single greatest archive of knowledge, the Library of Alexandria. Everything we thought we knew is now gone, and a new world of understanding must now be assembled, perhaps on a new track that recognizes that everything is oneness, there is no physical reality, there is only energy, all time is now, and everywhere is here. It's a new world.

28

La Vida es Para Sufrír

My Mexican grandmother, having seen suffering throughout her life, often expressed her philosophy about how to understand the meaning of life by saying, "La Vida es Para Sufrir," or "Life is for suffering."

This assertion brings us to a particular sticking point with skeptics, particularly those who have invested a great deal of their lives being faithful to their religion. That issue concerns the spiritual concepts of karma and reincarnation that were declared anathema by the Catholic Church in the Fourth Century and which was subsequently violently eradicated in the 13th century when Pope Innocent III formed an army to crush the competing Christian philosophy of Catharism. As you recall, hundreds of thousands of Christians—men, women, and children—suffered terribly as they were slaughtered to achieve this goal. Then, the inquisitors took over, rooting out anyone who had slipped through the war alive and forcing them to convert. This must have been a very important issue to suppress to go to such extremes to do so. Why? Power, of course. As long as the Priests were supreme, people had to go through them. Individuals couldn't work out their own karma or even reach God on their own.

Ironically, few Christians today are even aware that there ever was once a disagreement among early Christians regarding reincarnation. As a result, the topic is rarely discussed or introduced in Christian churches. They are equally ignorant about the Catholic Church's cover-up of the true story of Jesus as revealed in the Dead Sea Scrolls and in the Lost Gospels. Even worse, they are unaware that the scriptures they quote so often as the inerrant Word of God were tampered with by many unknown hands, the facts distorted, changed, or deleted to suit the current scribe's beliefs.

Scribes who copied the texts were sometimes biased zealots who were not concerned with accuracy or factual truth. At the very least, they may have changed the text to "improve the meaning" in order to make sense in their own time frame. Often, unknown writers wrote their own version of a Gospel and attached the name of an Apostle to make it seem authentic or more salable. Or, they may have been trying to modernize the language to their current day, but inadvertently changed the original meaning.

Many Christians today are also blissfully unaware that there are no original copies of the books on which they have staked their souls, and they continue to believe that the Bible is the inerrant word of God. Experts, like Dr. Bart Ehrman, who have read the many ancient texts in their original language, lost their faith and became atheists or agnostics because they discovered that the Bible is in no way the inerrant Word of God. If it were, there would not be so many errors and contradictions in it, even if some of the narratives contain bits of truth. In short, the Bible is not a reliable history book.

Ultimately, at the Councils of Constantine, the members had to guess which Gospel sounded as if it could have been penned by Matthew, Mark, Luke or John, and then blindly credit each one with a book that eventually was canonized in the New Testament.

Today, we have many issues confronting us, not the least of which is global climate change and its potentially existential consequences for life on Earth, as described by the beings to abductees all over the world. They have made it clear that the end may be near for all life on Planet Earth, as we seem to be in the midst of a major mass extinction event caused by humankind's mismanagement of Earth's resources. The beings report that they have been preparing for this outcome by collecting the DNA of all living things for reuse elsewhere if Planet Earth becomes uninhabitable. Additionally, they have been manufacturing a species that is more psychic, more intelligent, and more in tune with nature, a species that will succeed us if or when the time comes. These hybrids are already walking amongst us – I have met many in my travels. They look no different than any other human, but they are wise and aware of their roles in these troubled times.

I know this information is troubling, but with the little time we have left on this planet, before we destroy ourselves through war or by polluting the Earth to the point that it is no longer habitable, we should prepare for the day we die and meet the Archons face to face. How will we be judged? They already know everything there is to know about each of us. They have recorded every thought and action we have ever made, but there is still a little time to atone for our errors. There is still time to forgive our enemies and show love to our fellow humans. There is still time to disengage from the temptations of the physical world. There is still time to recover memories of our past lives. We should all use our limited time wisely and prepare.

No doubt some readers will remain skeptical of the material and amazing conclusions presented here. No one wants to believe that they are living in Hell, even though most people will admit that they have had hellish periods in their lives. Wars, genocide, natural disasters, pandemics, diseases, mass murders, serial killers, personal relationship issues and ultimately old age and death make for the perfect place to imprison souls.

Yes, of course, there are some beautiful moments in life and some people suffer less than others, but all in all, life on Planet Earth is short and often brutal. No one escapes without suffering the loss of a loved one, financial setbacks, anxiety and stress of some kind.

Now, in my old age, I reflect on how wise my grandmother was. She was right; I know because I have had my share of suffering, like feeling the agony of losing a child to suicide—that is true suffering.

There are two major religions that kept the idea of suffering and reincarnation in the forefront — Buddhism and Hinduism. Buddhism's basic tenets include the Five Precepts of karma, rebirth, mindfulness, compassion and dharma. Both Hinduism and Buddhism give power to their followers in how they can change their karma and hence, their suffering.

They, like my grandmother, believed that Life is suffering; suffering is caused by desire and attachment, and suffering can be ended by following the Eight-Fold Path, which is a set of Buddhist practices that guide people to end suffering, thus releasing them from the karmic wheel. They include the following:

>Right view: Understanding the nature of things, especially the Four Noble Truths
>
>Right intention: Avoiding harmful thoughts and intentions
>
>Right speech: Avoiding verbal misdeeds like lying and harsh speech
>
>Right action: Avoiding physical misdeeds like killing and stealing
>
>Right livelihood: Avoiding trades that harm others
>
>Right effort: Abandoning negative states of mind and sustaining a positive one
>
>Right mindfulness: Being aware of your body, feelings, thoughts, and phenomena
>
>Right concentration: Achieving single-mindedness

There are similar guidelines taught by Jesus that can prepare us for a better path ahead. Luckily for all of us, some of his greatest teachings survived the scribes and can inspire us all to do better and be kinder people.

For in the way you judge, you will be judged; and by your standard of measure, it will be measured to you. Why do you look at the speck that is in your brother's eye, but do not notice the log that is in your own eye? —Matthew 7:2-3

You shall love your neighbor as yourself. There is no other commandment greater than this." — Mark 13.31

The man who has two tunics is to share with him who has none; and he who has food is to do likewise. —Luke 3:11

Any kingdom divided against itself is laid waste; and a house divided against itself falls. —Luke 11:17

Therefore I say to you, all things for which you pray and ask, believe that you have received them and they will be granted you. —Mark 11:24

And even Jesus said, "For nothing is hidden that will not become evident, nor anything secret that will not be known and come to light. So take care how you listen; for whoever has, to him more shall be given; and whoever does not have, even what he thinks he has shall be taken away from him." —Luke 8:17

Years ago when I was working as a financial advisor, one of my clients referred an elderly Jewish man to me. As I did with all of my clients, I had a long talk with him about his life so as to understand his financial situation and needs.

I found out that he was a recently retired oncologist whose wife was ill. He explained that he was Polish and had served in the Army as a doctor during the Korean War. Then he said that there was something else that I should know. He rolled up his left sleeve and placed his hand on the table palm up. I could readily see a tattoo on his inner arm above his wrist—a series of numbers running up his arm.

"I don't understand," I said.

"I was liberated by the Americans from a Nazi concentration camp. This was my identification number. They gathered us all up and put us in cattle cars and shipped us to the death camps. I lost my parents and my brother and sister. None of them made it, and the young men were used as slave labor."

"That's just awful," I replied. "I don't know how you were able to live with those horrible memories. I'm so sorry."

"There was only one way to survive and continue living," he explained. "I forgave them all—Hitler, the Nazis, the guards, the soldiers who took my family. That was the only way."

I was stunned and amazed that someone could forgive such horrible acts. This example was one of the most important teachings that survived the editing of the Bible – we must always forgive one another. And it may be the most important aspect.

Then came Peter to him, and said, "Lord, how oft shall my brother sin against me, and I forgive him? till seven times?" And Jesus said to him, "I say not unto thee, until seven times: but, until seventy times seven." —Matthew 18:21-22

Here was a person who instinctively understood the power of forgiveness. Furthermore, although he had accumulated significant wealth, he lived modestly in a small house that he and his wife had purchased 50 years before. He didn't live extravagantly, and he told me that he wanted nothing more than to leave his wealth to his two daughters who needed the money more than he and his wife did. He remained my client for many years, and when he and his wife passed, I became his daughter's financial advisor.

I will always be grateful for the lessons he taught me, and I remain in awe of this tender man who was a living example of how we should all live our lives. I can't help but think now that karma was involved in helping him learn the lesson of unconditional love through many lifetimes. It would be difficult for a soul to become this advanced in one lifetime.

So what can we do to make our lives easier? To relieve our karmic debt? To get off the reincarnation wheel?

Whitley Strieber, once a devoted Catholic, recently told me: "The bottom line about reincarnation is this: If you don't believe in it, then you have no chance of ever escaping the cycle of reincarnation." And perhaps that is the purpose behind the Church's denial. The Church may not be an engine of resurrection at all, but an engine of soul entrapment.

Strieber left the Church and set out on his own spiritual journey, just as many have done, and in the process he helped many millions of people to deal with their own abduction experiences. Likewise, Mack left the safety of his, and his institution's accepted scientific paradigm and struck out on his search for truth and he also ended up helping millions of people.

In doing so, they did what is expected of us all – to find a way to help our fellow humans to find a path toward enlightenment. This path leads us out of the otherwise never-ending cycle of reincarnation on this planet.

No matter what our daily jobs entail, it is essential to find some way to devote time to tasks that help others. Some people volunteer to help those in need in their community, like the homeless. Another may donate a kidney to a dying stranger.

Acts of kindness are all around us. Many teachers and nurses go beyond what is expected of them and help others every day. You don't have to be a Christian to do the right things to get out of the reincarnation game.

The Gnostics lived in the Second Century CE and considered themselves Christians. However, the early church fathers denounced them as heretics for believing that they could achieve wisdom and insight without going through the church. They believed in the importance of attaining special, hidden knowledge (Gnosis) through spiritual enlightenment, which was not accessible to everyone. Gnosis means knowing. Spiritual enlightenment means knowing yourself.

Benjamin Franklin was wise. He once said that there are three things that are extremely hard—steel, a diamond, and to know one's self.

Today we know that exploring past lives, meditation and contemplation can all assist in knowing one's self.

Anyone who has received a "knowing" about an aspect or a particular experience of their life, will understand. The knowing is clear; it cannot be denied; and it moves you to the depths of your being. You just know. It is gnosis. But it is almost impossible to convey that knowledge to others. It is your special knowledge.

Through a gnostic experience I became convinced that I accompanied Jesus at the Essene community on the shores of the Dead Sea. This gnostic experience led me to believe that I am far more qualified today to interpret the ancient texts than any cleric.

Gnosis compels me to make such a bold statement.

So...what is *your* bold statement? Why are you here? What do you wish to accomplish? Is there a region or historical period that draws you to it? Do you need to learn something from that era? And how can you make the world around you better?

Oh, yes, there's one more thing to remember about Jesus. He was a powerful, immortal, angelic being who incarnated into the flesh to carry out a predetermined mission here on Earth....

Just like you!

About the Author
Dr. Joe Lewels

Francisco J. (Joe) Lewels, Jr. is the author of *Uses of the Media by the Chicano Movement: A Study in Minority Access.* (New York: Praeger Publishing, 1974); *The God Hypothesis: Extraterrestrial Life and Its Implications for Science and Religion.* (Mill Spring, N.C.: Wild Flower Press, 1996; second ed. 2005); *Rulers of the Earth: Secrets of the Sons of God.* (Lakeville, MN: Galde Press, Inc., 2007) and *On the Rio Grande: Stories from my Life on the Border.* (Hendersonville, N.C.: Galde Press, Inc. 2018).

Lewels served as a captain in the U.S. Army Corps of Engineers and as a reconnaissance pilot in the Republic of South Vietnam in 1967-1968. He was awarded the bronze star and the air medal with oak-leaf clusters for his service in combat.

He was a tenured associate professor and Chairman of the Departments of Journalism and Mass Communication at the University of Texas at El Paso from 1972-1982. He served as a consultant on minorities and the media at the U.S. Department of Justice and at the Federal Communications Commission in 1972-1973.

From 1982-2013 he was a Vice President and a Senior International Financial Advisor at Merrill Lynch. He edited the Freedom of Information Digest at the University of Missouri and was a writer and editor at the U.S. Army Aviation Digest at Ft. Rucker, Alabama.

From 1993 until 2000, Lewels served as Assistant State Director for West Texas and Southern New Mexico for the Mutual UFO Network (MUFON),. He regularly contributed to the *MUFON Journal* and spoke at many MUFON conferences and numerous international conferences in the United States and abroad.

He holds a Ph.D. in Journalism and Mass Communication from the University of Missouri, an M.S. in Education from Troy State University, and a B.A. in Journalism from Texas Western College. He was certified as a hypnotherapist by the American Board of Hypnotherapy in 1995.

Acknowledgements

I acknowledge and express my thanks and gratitude to the many people to whom I am indebted for their support and inspiration. These include Whitley Strieber, the late John E. Mack, MD., Linda Moulton Howe, Dr. Roberta Fennig, the late Robert O. Dean, the late Dr. Romeo Di Benedetto, Raymond Fowler, Barbara Lamb, and the many subjects of my research into the mystery of alien abductions, including Rita Perregrino, Shona Bear Clark, Joy Tarver, Melanie Young, Concepción Rodriguez, Dr. Soledad de la Peña, and many more.

You have been my teachers and supporters.

Thank you and bless you all.

Index

A

Abduction: Human Encounters with Aliens 9, 24, 25, 175
abduction phenomenon 21
Adam 62
Alabama 3
Albigensians 88
aliens 105, 137
Allegro, John 57
ancient documents 198, 199
Andreasson Affair 110
Andreasson Affair, Phase Two, 110
Andreasson Legacy 110
Antiquity of the Jews 47
Aramaic 50
Arianism 69
Arizona 192
Arkansas 19
Ascension 114
Augustine 75
Australia 7, 8, 10, 29

B

Beckwith, J. Carroll 185, 189
Ben-Joseph 150
Ben-Zachariah 149
Bhagavada Purana 45
Bhagavad Gita 45
Bible xiii, xiv, 10, 206, 210
Bigelow, Robert 201
Bohm, David 203
Bonnes Femmes 90
Bons Hommes 90
Book of Dzyan 176
book of "Q" 66
Bowman, Carol 182
Bram 94
Breakthrough 10

Bridge of Forgetfulness 43
Buchanan, Lynn 190
Buddhism 45, 208
Buddhists xv, 109

C

Caiaphas 64, 163
California 11
Cambodia 154, 160
Cannon, Dolores 138
Carcassonne 94
Cathari 89
Cathars xv, 90, 92, 96, 98, 109
Catholic 29
Catholicism 9, 11, 14, 28, 58, 206
Center for UFO Studies (CUFOS) 4
Chariots of the Gods 136
Children's Past Lives 182
China 102
Churton, Tobias 91
Close Encounters of the Third Kind 4
Communion 2, 4
Compact Bible Dictionary 146
Confirmation 10, 129
Constantine 68, 69, 71
Constantinople 87
Cosmic Game Wardens 133
Council of Constantinople 86
Council of Nicaea 68
Councils of Constantine 206
Crick, Francis 133
cross 57
Custodians: Beyond Abduction 138, 139

D

Dalai Lama 101, 103
dark matter and dark energy 109
David 48
Dead Sea 47, 48, 62
Dead Sea Scrolls 62, 143, 206
Dean, Command Sergeant Major Robert O. 157, 190
de la Peña, Dr. Soledad 117
Di Benedetto, Dr. Romeo 130
Directed Panspermia 135, 141
Division of Perceptual Studies 182
DNA 133, 134, 135, 137, 178
dogma 189
double helix 133, 197
Downing, Barry ix
Dragon Power 196
dragons 178
Dreamland 10
Dr. Romeo Di Benedetto 130
Druze 46

E

Ehrman, Dr. Bart 59
Eight-Fold Path 208
Einstein, Albert 152, 203
Elijah 52
Elizabeth 52
El Popo 118
Empedocles 43
Enki 195
Enoch 62, 148
Essenes xv, 47, 48, 56, 87, 109, 142, 150, 157
ET contact, ancient ix
Evil 112
extraterrestrials 105, 161, 169, 178

F

FBI 16
Fennig, Dr. Roberta 126, 129
Florida 158
Flying Serpents and Dragons 196
forgiveness 210
Fowler, Raymond 110, 113, 114
France 130
Franklin, Benjamin 212

G

Galilee 143
Gedun Drupa 101
Genesis 63
Ghirlandaio, Domenico 159
Glimpses of Other Realities 193
Gnosis 212
Gnostic Gospels 176
Gnostics xv, 87, 109
God Hypothesis 126, 175
Grays 22, 116
Greek 50
Grof, Dr. Stanislav 19, 179
Gui, Bernardo 97
Gurdjieff, George 5
Gyaincain Norbu 103

H

Harman, Michael 177
Harvard 18
Hinduism 208
Hopkins, Budd 1, 18
Howe, Linda Moulton 193
Hunchbacked Woman 182, 188
hybrids 32, 113, 161, 171, 207
Hynek, Dr. J. Allen 3
hypnosis 198
hypnotherapy 26, 132
hypnotic regression 27

I

identification number 210
implants 9
impregnation 9
Inquisition 96, 98, 99
Intruders 2

J

Jesus 66, 142, 157, 159, 212
Jesus and the Essenes 142
Jesus's name 57
John 73, 91, 206
John the Baptist 53
Josephus 66
Joshua 48
Judaism 143

K

Kabbalah 46
karma 42, 101, 189, 205
karmic wheel 208
Keepers of the Garden 140
Korea 158

L

Lamb, Barbara 25, 174, 181
Languedoc 93, 96
Laos 160
Lavaur 94
La vida es para sufrír 205
Lawrence of Arabia 181
Les Casses 94
Lethe 43
Lewels, Hilda 152
Library of Alexandria 204
Life After Life 182
Life Itself: its nature and origins 135
Looking for Carroll Beckwith 185

Lost Gospels 206
Lost Teachings of the Cathars 98
LSD 19, 134
Luca, Betty Andreasson 110
Luke 73, 206, 209

M

Mack, Dr. John 9, 10, 15, 17, 18, 21, 174, 190
Madonna 159
Mahabharata 45
mantis 116, 168, 193
Many Lives, Many Masters 106, 108
Mark 72, 206, 209
Marmande 94
Mary 48, 72, 160
Mary Magdalene 72, 73, 93
Masquerade of Angels 194
mass extinction 207
Masters 105
Matthew 53, 206, 209
McLain, Shirley 4
Meng Po 43
Messiah 131, 149
Mexico 7, 24, 116, 157, 162, 166, 190
Michigan 3
Milik, Fr. Josef 62, 63
Missouri 138, 152
Mnemosyne 43
Monfort, Count Simon de 95
Montesegur 94
Moody, Raymond 182
Moses 48
MUFON 190
Mutual UFO Network (MUFON) 20, 121, 139, 160

N

Nag Hammadi 75, 176
Name of the Rose 98
Narby, Jeremy 177
National Institute for Discovery Science (NIDS) 200
Native Americans 8
Nature's End 2
Nazareth 143
Nazi concentration camp 210
near-death experience (NDE) 124
Nevada 25, 181
New Mexico 191, 192
New Zealand 8
Nicene Creed 70
Nirvana 45
Noah 62
Nordics 116

O

Order No. 5 103
Origen 44
Orpheus 42
OVNIs 119

P

Passport to the Cosmos 21, 175, 179
Paulicianism 88
Pentecostal Church 110
Perfects 91
Perregrino, Rita 166
Peter 210
Pindar 43
Plato 44
Pope Innocent III 92, 93
Popocatepetl 117
Princeton 59
prisoners on our planet 6
Project Blue Book 3
Purposeful Universe 152

Q

Qumran 49, 62, 65, 144, 147, 148, 157

R

Ramirez, Dr. 163, 164
Raymond Fowler 110
recycle souls 1, 6
reincarnation 42, 43, 54, 86, 205
reptilians 166, 169, 170
Rice, Ted 194
Rodriquez, Concepción 191
Romans 47, 87, 92
Rosicrucians 46
Rulers of the Earth 8, 177

S

Sacred Congregation for the Doctrine of Faith 96
Sadducees 47
Salome 72
scientific method 199, 200
screen memories 9
scrolls 52, 57, 60, 62
Sermon on the Mount 131
Simon de Montfort, Count 94
Sitchin, Zechariah 195
Skinwalker Ranch 201
Smith, Andrew Phillip 90
Snow, Captain Robert L. 184, 189
Song of the Cathar Wars 94
Son of God 131
Souls 1
Soul Transfers 190
Soul Trap ix
South China Sea 155
spiritual 21
Sri Lanka 183
Stevenson, Dr. Ian 182
Strieber, Whitley 2, 7, 190, 211
Suddi 148, 150

Summoned: Encounters with
    Alien Intelligence 146
suspended animation 171
swamp gas 3

T

Tall Blondes 116, 129
Teacher of Righteousness 48, 50,
    54, 57, 145
telepathy 9
Texas 1, 4, 11, 15, 160, 190
The Believer 25
The God Hypothesis 8, 200
The Hunger 2
Theosophy 46
The Secret School 10, 12
The Threat 23
The UFO Experience 3
The Wolfen 2
Torah 144, 148
Transformation 10
Typhon 197

U

Unknown Country 10
U.S. Air Force 3

V

Vietnam 3, 156, 158, 160
Virginia 182
Visitors 6

W

Waldensians 96
Warday 2
Watchers 63, 110, 111, 203
Watchers II 110, 112
Way of the Shaman 178
Weiss, Dr. Brian 104, 113
When Time Began 195

Y

Yeshua of Yoshua 48

Z

Zechariah 52
Zeus 197

References

Allegro, John. *The Dead Sea Scrolls and the Christian Myth*. Buffalo, New York: Prometheus Books, 1992.

"Ancient Theories of the Soul." *Encyclopedia of Philosophy*. 2024.

Barnstone, Willis, ed. *The Other Bible*. San Francisco: Harper, 1984. (Author's note: All quotes from the Dead Sea Scrolls and The Gnostic Gospels are to be found in Barnstone's *The Other Bible*.)

Baigent, Michael, and Richard Leigh. *The Dead Sea Scrolls Deception*. New York: Touchstone, 1991.

Bergmark, Janet. *In the Presence of Aliens*. St. Paul, MN: Llewelyn Publications, 1997.

Bhaktivedanta, A.C., *Bhagavad-Gita As it Is*. New York: The Bhaktivedanta Book Trust, New York, 1972.

Bohm, David. *Quantum Theory*. Englewood Cliffs, NJ: Prentice-Hall, Inc. 1951.

Boulay, R.A. *Flying Serpents and Dragons*. Clearwater, FL: Galaxy Books, 1990.

Bowman, Carol. *Children's Past Lives: How Past Life Memories Affect Your Child*, Bantam Books, 1997.

Bremmer, J. *The Early Greek Concept of the Soul*. Princeton: Princeton University Press, 1983.

Bryant, T. Alton. *Zondervan Compact Bible Dictionary*. Nashville, TN: Zonderfan

Burrows, Millar. *The Dead Sea Scrolls*. New York: The Viking Press, 1955.

Bramley, William. *The Gods of Eden*, San Jose, CA: Dahlin Family Press, 1989.

Cannon, Dolores. *Jesus and the Essenes*, Bath, UK: Gateway Books, 1992.

_____. *The Custodians*, Huntsville, AR: Ozark Mountain Publishing, 1998.

Carpenter, John. "Reptilians and Other Unmentionables," *MUFON UFO Journal*, April, 1993, pp.10-11.

Charles, James H., ed. *Jesus and the Dead Sea Scrolls*. New York: The Anchor Bible Reference Library, 1992.

Charles, R.H. (ed.) *The Books of the Secrets of Enoch*. Oxford: Clarendon Press, 1896.

Chase, David. *A Visual Guide to Alien Beings*. Seattle, WA: David Chase, 1995.

Churton, Tobias. *The Gnostics*. New York: Barnes & Noble, 1997.

Cooper, John M. (ed.) *Plato, Complete Works*. Indianapolis: Hackett Publishing Co., 1997.

Crick, Francis. *Life Itself*. New York: Simon and Schuster, 1981.

Cross, Frank M. *The Ancient Library of Qumran and Modern Biblical Studies*. Grand Rapids, Mich.: Baker Book House, 1980.

Downing, Barry H. *The Bible and Flying Saucers*, Philadelphia, PA: J.B Lippencott Co. 1968.

Ehrman, Bart D. *Misquoting Jesus: The Story Behind Who Changed The Bible and Why*. New York: Harper One, 2005.

Eisenman, Robert, and Michael Wise. T*he Dead Sea Scrolls Uncovered*. Rockport, MA: Element, 1992.

Eusebius. *The History of the Church*. London: Penguin Books, 1965.

Fowler, Raymond E. *The Watchers*. New York: Bantam Books, 1990.

_____*The Andreasson Affair*. Mill Spring, NC: Wild Flower Press, 1994.

_____*The Watchers II*. Mill Spring, NC: Wild Flower Press, 1995.

Grant, Michael. *Constantine the Great,The Man and His Times*, New York: Barnes and Noble, Inc., 1993.

Grof, Stanislov. *The Holotropic Mind*. San Francisco, CA: Harper, 1992.

_____. *The Adventure of Self Discovery*. Albany, N.Y.: State University of New York Press, 1988.

Harner, Michael. *The Way of the Shaman*. New York: Harper and Row, 1980.

Head, Joseph and Cranston, S. I. *Reincarnation: An East-West Anthology*. New York: The Julian Press, 1961.

Hendel, Ronald S. "When the Sons of God Cavorted with the Daughters of Men" from *Understanding the Dead Sea Scrolls,* edited by Hershel Shanks. New York: Random House, 1992.

Hopkins, Budd. *Intruders*. New York: Ballantine Books, 1987.

The Holy Bible, King James Version.

Howe, Linda Moulton. *Glimpses of Other Realities, High Strangeness, Vol. II.,* LMH Productions Albuquerque, NM *1993*.

Jacobs, David. *The Threat; Revealing the Secret Alien Agenda*. New York: Simon and Schuster, 1999.

Lamb, Barbara and Nadine Lalich. *Alien Experiences*. Victoria, BC. Canada: Trafford Publishing, 2008.

Laurence, Richard. *The Book of Enoch the Prophet*. San Diego: Wizards Bookshelf, 1998.

Lewels, Joe Ph.D. *The God Hypothesis: Extraterrestrial Life and its Implications for Science and Religion,* 2d ed. Mill Spring, N.C.: Wild Flower Press, 2005.

_____*Rulers of the Earth: Secrets of the Sons of God*. Lakeville MN: Galde Press, 2007.

Lorenz, H. "Plato on the Soul," *The Oxford Handbook on Plato*, G. Fine (ed.) Oxford: Oxford University Press, 1999.

Mack, Burton L. *The Lost Gospel of Q and Christian Origins*. New York: Harper Collins, 1994.

Mack, John E. M.D. *Abduction: Human Encounters with Aliens*. New York: Ballantine Books, 1995.

_____. *Passport to the Cosmos*. New York: Crown Publishers, 1999.

Manchester, William. *A World Lit Only by Fire*. New York: Little Brown and Company, 1993.

Meurois-Givandan, Anne and Daniel. T*he Way of the Essenes: Christ's Hidden Literature Remembered*. Rochester, VT.: Destiny Books, 1993.

Milik, Joseph, ed. *The Books of Enoch*. Oxford: Clarendon Press, 1976.

Moody, Raymond. *Life After Life: The Investigation of a Phenomenon— Survival of Bodily Death,* New York: Mockingbird Books (Ballantine Books) , 1975.

Moulton Howe, Linda, *Glimpses of Other Realities Vol. II*. New Orleans: Paper Chase Press, 1998.

Narby, Jeremy. *The Cosmic Serpent*. New York: Jeremy P. Tarcher/Putnam, 1998.

Pagels, Elaine. *The Gnostic Gospels*. New York: Random House, 1979.

Puryear, Herbert Bruce. *Why Jesus Taught Reincarnation*. Scottsdale, AZ: New Paradigm Press, 1992.

Radin, Dean. *Entangled Minds: Extrasensory Experiences in a Quantum Reality*. New York: Pocket Books, 2006.

Redfield, Dana. *Summoned: Encounters with Alien Intelligence Hampton Roads, VA, 1999.*

Shanks, Hershel, ed. *Understanding the Dead Sea Scrolls*. New York: Random House, 1992.

Sitchin, Zecharia. *When Time Began*. New York: Avon Books, 1990.

_____. *The Wars of Gods and Men*. New York: Avon Books, 1985.

Snow, Robert. *Looking for Carroll Beckwith*. Emmaus, PA: Daybreak Books, 1999.

Smith, Andrew Phillip. *The Lost Teachings of the Cathars*. London: Watkins, 2015.

Stevenson, Ian. *Where Reincarnation and Biology Intersect,* Westport CT, Praeger Publishers, 1*997.*

Strieber, Whitley. *Communion*. New York: Beech Tree Books, 1987.

_____. *The Secret School*. New York: Beech Tree Books, 1996.

Talbot, Michael. *Beyond the Quantum*. New York: Bantam Books, 1988.

_____*The Holographic Universe*. New York: Harper Collins, 1991.

Tehart, Franjo, and Janina Schulze. *World Religions.* Bath, UK: Paragon Publishing, 2013.

Turner, Karla. *Masquerade of Angels.* Roland AR.: Kelt Works, 1994.

USA Today. "Human Cloning: Unsettling and Now Perhaps Inevitable." Feb. 25, 1997, p. 14A.

Weiss, Brian. *Many Lives, Many Masters.* New York: Simon and Schuster, 1998.

Wigoder, Geoffrey, general ed. *Illustrated dictionary and Concordance of the Bible.* Jerusalem: G.G. The Jerusalem House Publishers, 1986.

Documenting the Unexpected...
Wild Flower Press,
An imprint of
Granite Publishing L.L.C.
P.O. Box 338
Mount Pleasant, SC 29464

All our books are available through

Amazon.com

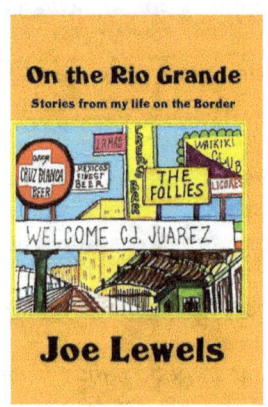

On the Rio Grande:
Stories From My Life on the Border,
2018

Comments from Amazon readers for past books:

2005

- Much of the history we are being taught...needs serious revision.... Buy this book !!!

- What a thought-provoking book! An easy read and hard to put down for a thinking pause!

- Very interesting and well written. Well worth the mind-expanding read. I bought this book... and immediately started reading it. Now, after years of personal and spiritual growth, I must read it again. This book feels so right....
Thank you Mr. Lewels!

- Great read! I strongly recommend this awesome book to anyone who is searching for truth with an open mind.

2013

- Lewels has written another excellent book. I bought 30 of them to share with my friends.

- Very informative! He changed my life. I loved his thoughts on both the Old Testament/Punishing and Cruel God, and the New Testament/Kind, Forgiving God. He made a very good case that the Old and New Testament Gods could very well have been different. The book changed my paradigm, It is a must read.

- ...the best researched and most thought-out book on (alien?) abductions I've read to date. No matter how much you've read on the subject, there are things here that will make you say "hmmm".

www.ingramcontent.com/pod-product-compliance
Lightning Source LLC
Chambersburg PA
CBHW071905290426
44110CB00013B/1285